New Life

Also by Dan O'Brien

Poems
War Reporter
Scarsdale

Plays
The Body of an American
The Cherry Sisters Revisited
The Disappearance of Daniel Hand
The House in Hydesville
The Last Supper Restoration
The Voyage of the Carcass

New Life

Dan O'Brien

Hanging Loose Press
Brooklyn, New York

Published by Hanging Loose Press, 231 Wyckoff Street, Brooklyn, New York 11217-2208. All rights reserved. No part of this book may be reproduced without the publisher's written permission, except for brief quotations in reviews.

www.hangingloosepress.com

Originally published in UK by CB Editions, 2015

Printed in the United States of America
10 9 8 7 6 5 4 3 2 1

Hanging Loose Press thanks the Literature Program of the New York State Council on the Arts for a grant in support of the publication of this book.

Acknowledgments
Many of these poems have been previously printed in the following magazines: 32 Poems, Ambit, Bare Fiction, Cossack Review, California Journal of Poetics, The Charnel House (Bridgedoor Press), Consequence, Cyphers, The Fiddlehead, Hanging Loose, The Interpreter's House, Magma, Missouri Review, The Moth, The North, North American Review, Poetry Ireland Review, Poetry Wales, The Rialto, Sonofabook, Stand, The Stinging Fly, storySouth, Subtropics, Sugar House Review, The Sunday Times, Troubadour Poetry Prize 2014 winner, UCity Review, War, Literature & the Arts, Warwick Review, Yale Review

ISBN 978-1-934909-86-7

Library of Congress cataloging-in-publication available on request.

Contents

To Jessica and to Isobel—to our new life.

The realization that life is
absurd cannot be an end,
but only a beginning.

—Albert Camus

The War Reporter Paul Watson Recalls the Night Stalker

A soldier in every generation
since brother slew brother. So he enlists
in the tribe that lives to kill by the creed
that God will whisper your name to missions
insurmountable. Insurmountable,
yet like Christ harrowing the gates of Hell
the reward's another descent. Swearing
he'll save by savagery, knowing full well
one's truest friends are the night and the arts
of deception. *The gunman's legs dangled
from the doorsill. The belly of the bird
was charcoal. When a shoulder-launched grenade
mangled the gearbox, screwing the Black Hawk
into Mogadishu.* That's the picture
that wins the Pulitzer, Paul. *Look at it
at your leisure.* She's kicking him. *She is.*
He's beating him with a cane. Yes. Laughing.
The world has found its frame. And you're looking
at yourself. And we are violating
whatever made us human. And I hear
a voice as clear as yours, clearer even,
saying: *If you do this I will own you
forever.* Forgive me, just understand
I don't want to do this. No. We have to
do this. Yes. We have to do this until
we don't.

The Poet in Afghanistan

What do you say, my friend? All that's required
is the coin for Charon's fare. To Kabul
if Kandahar's too far. Why not reserve
your seat online? a window if like me
you enjoy your scenery. But steer clear
of Afghan Air. Tears in the fuselage
reveal a Mediterranean blur
blending into olive then khaki scree
howling into the head. *The breaking news
from Kabul spooks the poet.* The Inter
-Continental Hotel penetrated
by Haqqani transfiguring themselves
into dervishes of light that engulf
weddings mid-song, mid-step. Journalists jump
out of windows. While the poet schmoozes
a diplomat in the Nations Cafe
on Second Ave, the East River snaking
between brick face. Reminding the poet
of jogging past Bellevue, the smear of bone
in that Indian summer dusk. Advice
about Afghanistan? the speechwriter
asks the poet: Don't go. *The best hotels
are colonial, the war reporter
writes to the poet.* Kevlar vests laid out
like terrycloth robes, helmets like roses
or chocolates on pillows. A cellar full
of new wine. Where we'll hold court like David
Nivens in wicker chairs, ornamental
grasses between us. Ceiling fan ticking
like history. Interviewing Najib
for our next work of art. *The breaking news,
writes the poet to the war reporter,
is we're expecting.* Hard to imagine

myself as a father. And my wife's friend
just died of cancer. Hard to imagine
she's gone. Which is all to say I don't know
if the timing's exactly right. *Congrats!*
writes the war reporter. And anyway
Najib won't write back. Maybe he's escaped
to Pakistan? or had his hands hacked off
for interpreting me. But have no fear,
partner of mine. We'll find our new story
elsewhere in the meantime.

What the War Reporter Won't Tell the Poet the Poet Won't Tell the War Reporter

What about your wife, is she the reason
you're surviving? You never mention her
except to say she's the strongest woman
you've ever known. Just like your mother is
marmoreal for weathering the untimely
passing of your father. I guess. *We paused*
at Le Frolic *in Yellowknife. Halfway*
home to Rome the evergreens revived. Gas
-fire licking the hearth. Edmonton salesmen
wangling mud diamonds. Sawing through T-bone
steaks while a First Nations junkie swan dived
in a plowbank. Safety lights blinkering
Drug Mart with such lovely menace. Vodka's
my medicine of choice, Paul slurped fondue
chinoise. Your wife's Chinese, right? *I don't talk*
about her for a reason. Years slip by
before I'm haunting her kitchen listening
to her decry American destroyers
poisoning the South China Sea. The filament
of your son acing English, the mystery
of a father below threading pop songs
through the ether of his vernal reward
on a brilliant new device. Who could know
what would be waiting there for you? *Clenching*
through pugilistic wind to the Hotel
Explorer, this strangely swank, faux-Soviet
high-rise for diplomats. I don't know if
I'll still be married next year. I don't know
if you'll still be alive, or I will. Love
beyond reason is the reason for what

neither of us dared mention. I'm going
to Resolute soon, where the American
scientists migrate each summer. *I can't hear
you, Paul!* I said I'm doing a story
about robot submarines! searching for
lost Arctic explorers! *Maybe I'll try
for a grant to go with you?*

The War Reporter Paul Watson Expects to Depart

as soon as the body armor arrives
from Dallas. Ha ha ha. On backorder
after that latest culling of school kids
in your country. After reassurance
my next decent into the mouth of war
would be green-lit, reassurance I'd need
in order to take that psychic leap, X
Editor mentions O by the way Y
Editor's got the final say. Money
figures in the debate, unspeakably
of course. Insurance, I suppose. Truth is
Editors XY&Z are afraid
their soy lattes will sour at the news
one of their war reporter's been kidnapped
on their dime. We spend so much of our time
criticizing presidents and generals
who feed school kids into the mouth of war
when what we should do is just pause and check
the courage of our own decisions. Well
I checked mine, and it's my wife and my son
who are the courageous ones. And now's when
these assholes dither. If I'm beheaded
in Syria, editors and anchors
claiming to know me will offer up self
-serving sound bites. But you actually *do*
know me, Dan! So I'll tell my wife to send
all enquiries your way. I was venting
last night and she asked, Why not stop? No more
war. What would you do then? And I told her,
I'd fly to Hollywood and write a script
about war with Dan. But what do I know
about entertainment? Word is we'll hit
Aleppo next week. Hoping to come back
with some killer, high-concept anecdotes
sure to cinch our pitch.

The War Reporter Paul Watson Bids His Joy Farewell

Over FaceTime with his son complaining
about math, the cat's diarrhea, those dire
choral concerts, Paul mentions he'll be gone
a week or so. So what? ripostes his son
with a wit half his age. Knowing full well
no WiFi is murder. To Syria,
Paul persists. The betrayal. The Youngbloods
on his laptop, *We are but a moment's*
sunlight fading in the grass. His joy asks,
Why do you have to? Stay home. Twisting off
-screen to strangle his tears in the window's
vale of skiers. Paul's hotel glass unveils
a surf at Bourj Hammoud the squalor of
the scotch in his tumbler. The near-future
will often bleed through. Like this nine-year-old
girl in a hospital because shrapnel
from a mortar bomb pierced the tent and speared
an aluminum vessel like a balloon
atop their space heater. The flaming oil
splashed over her cheek, her arm. Her mother
tried to smother the screaming but only
smeared the searing goo farther. In an ear
that seemed to disappear. Now like a stone
moldered over with the moss of silver
sulfadiazine cream, caked on to ward off
sepsis. Fracturing like plaster. The ungloved
nurses peel the gauze. Assad's bombardment
reminds the city. The half-deaf girl's sobs
chasten a crowded hallway. This moment
gets photographed tomorrow. *I'll return*
soon, Paul promises. But in case I don't
make it back, all you'll need to do is go
up the mountainside and ask the forest

whether to ask out that girl. Ask the rain
how to finesse your mother. Ask the storm
if you can borrow His car. They're laughing
between their screens. *Can you promise?* His son
gambles, Fuck off. The song on Paul's laptop
switches to something less meaningful as
they disconnect.

The War Reporter Paul Watson to the Readers from Aleppo

Humor's as common as blood on the street
outside the restaurant Al-Quds, Arabic
for Jerusalem. Bat-like chickens roast
in respiring flames. For broken spirits
without power. The shape in the doorway
bellows, Every time you reporters come
al-Assad bombs us! Forgive me! I cry
before I see the shadows are laughing
at me. This man too. While delivering
through the door his bundle like a football
wrapped in greasy newspaper. *Bones sucked clean*
of their measly meat around the corner
at this desolate clinic. A snarling
boom shifts the room, and my fixer suggests
the cellar. I say we have a saying
in Canadian: Lightning never strikes twice
as the door's kicked open and barking men
are delivering the lowing heap of
that joker who gave me chicken. Naked
feet micturating blood. Eyes in the gas
-generated fluorescent light don't see
me, his double, focused between shoulders
on track suits, stonewashed denim. Blood that's spat
on linoleum. Snailed ointment tubes, husks
of gauze wrappers. A two-way radio
squawks the driver's hand to life. Blood-brined cheeks
had been bobbing as if dozing. A gay
nurse in his pink-collared sweater swaddles
the chicken-man, heel to toe. *Dear readers,*
I would remind myself to remind you
to pay attention. But I was the one
lusting for chicken. Which is why I missed
the point of this joke in the dark.

The War Reporter Paul Watson Reviews *Argo*

En route with an Afghan surgeon to see
his kid sister in Ottawa. The bridge
of his nose split like a prizefighter, scabs
glistening, bruises like port wine birthmarks
stain his face and arms. *Because the surgeon
was driving home at night.* Behind a cart
piled with plumbing pipes. When a motorbike
slips alongside, the man on back tossing
a hand grenade against the surgeon's half
-open window. Bouncing off the glass it
flashes in the road, makes a crystal hash
of the windshield in a shower that cuts
that gash in the surgeon's nose as he reels
in his fishtailing wheel. The man on back
fires two shots mid-swerve, as the surgeon's car
plows through the pipe-cart on its way into
a concrete wall. The would-be assassins
splutter down an alleyway. *Kandahar
is collapsing, finally.* Surgeries
from dusk till dawn and back again. So try
to help him decompress, Paul. Smile. Practice
in your mirror so you might seem unscarred,
psychologically. A hermit's hovel
is a dream you both share. Life in the mouth
of caves in these snow-Byzantine forests
you tumult through. Under cantilevered
rafters at the station, his sister speaks
English only somewhat better. You ask,
Would you care to see a movie? Pupils
dilating. *We have never.* They lean in
transfixed, flexing at the execution
sequences. Their father with the bullet
hole in the dome of his forehead is still

on their minds, of course. With these heroes snagged
at the Tehran airport, she's taken back
to her exodus last year. By the end
she's beaming like a witch in the flickering
fire of the screen, on the edge of her seat
conjuring that airplane into the air
with her arms outstretched. It's a moment, Soon
to become my story. The second time
I've seen this film, and still I find myself
crying, and much more than those characters
probably deserve.

The War Reporter Paul Watson Takes Some Afghans to Niagara

A force mightier than war. Heard falling
sideways underfoot and over the cusp
of everything and nothing, inspiring
rainbows in its pillowing haze. While limbs
emerge black through sheaths of ice. Dun grass breaks
through scabrous snow. *Aprille.* With pilgrims' breath
unfurling at the railing and the wind
beating up my mike. Plastic scraps whistling
in the razor wire of thorn bushes like
opium poppies. So we descend to view
the punishing wheel, foam specks floating, light
winking through epaulets on Sayed's shirt
while suspicious parents sandbag children
between their bellies. When Roya sneezes
she finds herself speaking English: *I beg
your pardon.* Elevating to the roar
above, again, flags flapping, peering through
coin-operated eyes at our allies
on the other side. *It's so much smaller
than in all the pictures.* I fell asleep
driving them home that night. When the rumble
strip woke us up—another tragedy
averted.

The War Reporter Paul Watson Visits the House of Commons

When Roya grows up she wants to become
a politician, which is a blood sport
where she's from. The Usher of the Black Rod
read my stories, then dutifully dug up
some funds. Her finest moment was speaking
about the need to speak. Afterwards sat
in the ornate, fern-velvet throne. All hail
the Queen! the security guard announced
as she bolted, blushing and relishing
her transgression. That tower like Big Ben
chiming provincially. Her brother shocked
by what is absent: Where are the soldiers
and concrete blast walls? Your country belongs
to everyone! he said as we ambled
the Rivière des Outaouais. Young lovers
conspiring on benches. The tricky path
through muddy fields. This is a good country
of good people, he said. Let's see, I said,
our tax dollars at work! while purchasing
tickets at the kiosk. Nothing happens
on a Friday, it turns out. Questioners
stung each other lazily. Where is she?
he asked. I thought she'd still be here. Checking
in early for the first flight of many
back to Kandahar, his sister ensconced
in boarding school, he finds himself asking
a stranger to borrow her cell. He spoke
to his sister gently, the onlooker
informs the reporter. *Then Dr. Shams*
returned the phone, said thank you and passed through
security easily. Though I don't think
he'll ever come back to this country, if
you ask me.

The Poet's Annus Mirabilis

On the 13th day of the sickest month
my brother threw himself out the window
of our house. So poetry. Crows and snow
in tight rhyme. And ever since that number's
been reforming. Like a flight into Eire
on a 13th in my youth. Conceiving
in the 13th year of this malignant
century. As I went out a-roving
one morning in a coastal fog, a voice
tells me I've been chosen. *But tell me why
must it always end sadly?* Promise me
you won't write about me, she'd ask. Promise
you'll keep your hands clean. Promise you'll study
the metrics of disease. Promise you'll hear
the phantom of your brother vomiting
in the bones of our house. Because sorrow
is hands, is breath. Because you and I, Paul,
are similar. We can't help but suspect
good fortune's a sentence to outlast while
failure's our mother saying, I will wait
for all my children to come crawling back
home to me. Then rolls the dice. *So we'll try
to get through this together.* Soldiering
through the fumes and slick of the sickest month
past that shop on Broadway where you purchased
shoes to replace the disintegrating
shoes of Rwanda. Your fingernails rimmed
with refugees' germs. Just as I've believed
one's sins sleep like seeds under another
bout of winter. My brother's body pressed
with snow, blades of dead grass. The light changes
Stop to Walk as I step from the curb struck
that he lived, lives now. While I'm accepting

the prize. You don't remember that day well,
Paul, and neither do I. Mostly I said
my wife was at home, sick with expecting
our new life.

The War Reporter Paul Watson Paraphrases *The Decameron*

O memorable mortality! begins
the beginning. In medieval something
or other. Mine eyes have seen the gory
bloat of bodies. Swine thumbing through pockets
with sweaty penis-like snouts, then dropping
dead in the scrum of a heartbeat. Some fled
indoors to their assault rifles. Shunning
their fat wives, watching cable news. Fingering
the blinds to spy on the carts rattling
corpses towards their dirt naps. While others
avouched there was no physic more sovereign
than jet-skiing. By their revels mocking
children who spray blood with breath. In between
these antipodes there were still others
gathering nosegays in vellum hands, herbs
odoriferous, potpourris of cocaine
pressed to facelifts. Escaping to chalets
in Stowe, or Chamonix-Mont-Blanc, as if
the hands of Death embraced only the swine
of Kabul or Homs. Whereupon the Queen
proclaims, Let each man relate whatever
tale he finds most diverting. And turning
to me and you, Dan, she nods it is time
we begin.

The War Reporter Paul Watson Pitches the Drama

She likes combat sex. Bouncing in the back
of Humvees, inappropriately jerking
around her band of brothers. Just one more
type-A indefatigable misfit
estranged from family in Hong Kong who prize
their disappointment in her. She's serene
in fire fights, swearing like a Teamster when
she has to bust his balls. An IED
blasts them into bed, where they fall in love
even though she knows she won't be able
to keep his baby. *He woos her with poems*
secreted in his Moleskine. His Master
of Fine Arts from Yale School of Drama, Bard
for his Bachelor's. His correspondent dad
dead of deep vein thrombosis, he dresses
fastidiously for him. Floating on streams
of unconscious dread. In due course he'll win
a Pulitzer with his wife. *Their divorce*
will be mostly due to this ingénue
past her sell-by date. Who buys her Canon
on Amazon used, catapults herself
into war zones. Concerned about desert
winds drying her out, she lathers lotion
into bare shoulders. Terrorists ogling
like schoolboys, grinning daggers. So she spreads
it on thicker next time. *He's a lone wolf*
with PTSD. Secluding himself
in his dreary sublet in Bourj Hammoud
with an ocean view, a tumbler of scotch
in hand. Pursued by JPEGs of phantoms
in camouflage, dog tags as winkling wind
chimes, 9 mm slipped in his mouth
for the taste sometimes. Wants out. Gets offered

a career in Hollywood, or PR,
but he'd rather get kidnapped than get paid
to lie more than he already does. Years
of SSRIs have taken their toll
on his libido, but still he can rise
to most occasions, when inspired. *The spy*
feeds him her party lies. As they promenade
along the Corniche, sunset spume flirting
between barrier rocks. She'll pick his brain
out of her pillow. Delivering the news
along encrypted lines, she falls in lust
with the hunky addict next. *Who survives*
paradoxically thanks to Bob Capa's
dictum: If your pictures suck you're not close
enough. To paraphrase. This very same
philosophy he follows when stalking
his nightly barroom prey. That signature
fetid keffiyeh without fail, necklaced
with cameras, wide-angle to phallically
telephoto. He turns heads. She wants me
to fuck her, he likes to grunt. In the port
-o-john on base. Just like he brags about
his dalliances with death. So naturally
no one will share a cab with him. Either
he's a natural, or a natural
psychopath. Who tends to become a gay
-basher when drunk. So no surprise he longs
for his fixer. *This swashbuckling Christian*
Beiruti, inventively elusive
of rebel militia. Israel's Thunder
fighters flattened his father's glue factory
in '06, so he needs dollars to rent
his industrial-chic, metal-façaded
condo in Hamra. Where professors roll
backgammon by day, by night transvestites

in leather minis, thigh-high boots parade
like Brigitte Bardots. He's not too halal,
but every American woman's a snake
to be charmed, then crushed. *Twice-divorced, the plague
of her profession.* Brittle, she resents
the passion of her charges. This doyenne
of the bureau on Rue Bliss. A frat house
with a feline touch, a couch for flopping
and fucking, keepsakes like casings. Paranoid
she'll get fired, she digs through his duffel and
unlocks his device. Pilfering explicit
texts to forward to his wife. True motives
aside, she's a heroine hammering
her sensible haircut against the glass
ceiling, while still coddling and coaxing dicks
who hold the purse strings. *Those Rear Echelon
Mother Fuckers.* In his fishbowl office
armored with diplomas and photographs
of prestigious handshakes. The Rainmaker
sips immaculately. Slipping away
early. Try to lead with that teen blowjob
story, he'll say. He'd rather be sailing
but he's monastic, knees blown out leaping
from hovering Hueys in sweltering delta
LZs. Answering the phone when they call
to tell him his surrogate son's been lost
in the streets of Aleppo as gas sweeps
in scentless on breezes. He's no different
from those generations of snow-haired men
sending generations of wheat-haired boys
into the thresher of war. *A healer
-cum-psychiatrist in a back alley
room sweet with sandalwood.* Sitar, tabla
splashing off his laptop. His voice soothing,
his wink impish. Our Magic Indian's

an immigrant to Lebanon. Pseudo
-mystical about life. The water pipe
on the ottoman leaves the impression
he's half-stoned most of the time. In a world
sick with killing, he's a glutton failing
to follow his own advice to pay heed
to nobler truths, the most helpful of which
reminds us that war is the light that's thrown
from the burning wick of desire.

The War Reporter Paul Watson on the Downward Slope

Over tea with the Movie Producer
and the Poet, the War Reporter breathes
in the majestic view from this third-floor
patio of a mock-Spanish Gothic
villa pronounced *Karma.* Cracks patched after
Loma Prieta. A satellite dish
astride the hills like SETI, with hikers
wayfaring through faerie grasslands, rumored
habitat of the endangered tiger
salamander. Horseflies on teacups like
*The Decameron. If only they'd get
what I'm saying,* says the War Reporter
—*then* we'd live differently. We're here and then
—*poof.* The Movie Producer's skeptical:
Yes, but. You know I'm on the precipice,
the War Reporter ventures, of making
T-shirts that proclaim, Love is a method
of revolution! I like that! applauds
the Producer as she rolls up a sleeve
of turquoise bracelets. Did you make that up
or nick it from someone? I made it up
and I believe it. Well I would just love
to find a way to get those T-shirts made
for you! laughs the Producer. Why don't we
make some real money then? the Reporter
laughs rubbing his hands together. Let's shoot
a movie, like a rom-com? —Ha ha ha,
snorts the Poet who until this moment
hasn't had much to say. Oh by the way,
says the Producer, I happened to tell
X who'll be writing the screenplay—Who's X?
asks the War Reporter, the Memoirist
of the source material for the opera

the Poet wrote the libretto for, and
now this film, apparently. Actually
you had a long conversation with X
many moons ago, the Producer jogs
the Reporter's memory. And he promised
he'd try and join us for lunch, at least brunch,
but X's father's been on the downward
slope for like months. And I'm like, X—come *on!*
And he's like, *What?* my father's retreated
to San Carlos. And I'm all, Where the hell
is San Carlos? And he goes, On the Sea
of Cortez. So I say, Where is the Sea
of Cortez? even though I don't care if
it's the Sea of Fucking Galilee—when
the Memoirist's in town the Screenwriter
comes to lunch! Or brunch, at least. Ha ha ha,
the Poet and the War Reporter glance
at each other terrified. But I don't
say that, she says. I say, X, let me know
when things change. So. Whatever. However
you mentioned, one of you mentioned? something
about pitching a TV show and X
won an Emmy and a Golden Globe and
he can walk this thing right into Playtone
today. What's Playtone? asks the Poet. Tom
Hanks, sniffs the Producer. Because I *love*
your story, Paul. As you know. And I *know*
Tom would love it too, and so would Spielberg.
Who's Spielberg? smiles the War Reporter. *When*
the lights have dimmed on an atonal life
the Poet drives the War Reporter home
to their hotel. Your lyrics have captured
what I've never, he flatters. *Unbuckling*
seat belts, gathering luggage. Librettos
wrinkled in armpits. My brother was found

dead last night, he says. In his apartment.
He was obese, a recluse. His neighbors
noticed the smell. He'd been on the downward
slope since the day he was born. And truth is
I hardly feel a thing! I've felt more grief
taking pictures of corpses. That opera
tonight of my life has made me feel more
than my own brother's death. But that's no shock,
I guess. Music is peaceful, especially
all that singing.

The War Reporter Paul Watson after the Opera

—'s a big difference between facts and the truth,
slurs the buzzed Tenor. On the hotel porch
campy with Tiki torches. The courtyard
bloats our vowels, the pool glowers. A clutch
of show-folk beneath the palms. While countless
Somalis festered outside the frame, booms
our Basso Profondo. I don't want to
get too personal, the Tenor's protesting
too much, because I performed You and You
are sitting here right now! —I don't even
like my name! laughs Paul. And we were singing
like, Paul! Paul! all night long! the Soprano
pierces the throng. Can I get anyone
anything else to drink? the Mexican
waiter mumbles. Last call. I'll have one more,
says Paul. *Make that two.* The busboy finger
-spears a chorus of empties. And pardon
my French, says the Tenor, cause I've fucked up
my life too, but when you called that soldier's
mom, I'm like, *What?* —You see? says Paul, that's fact,
but your performances told us the Truth
outside the frame! Ha ha ha! modesty
gushing from singers. O believe me! O
believe me! I'm sitting there watching Me
and thinking, You ass! If only we'd known
you were coming tonight—boo! spews the Bass
languidly. We thought we had another
night, the Countertenor translates. I wept
for myself, Paul confesses. You wanted
to be forgiven, soothes the Baritone
with gravity. No, I wanted to be
elevated. Transfigured. And fact is
that's conceited. That's pathetic. That's art,

whispers the Soprano into her glass
of ice. That's *true*, says Paul, as the waiter
brings our final round.

The War Reporter Paul Watson Hears Some Phantom Words

A visiting British psychologist
is looping two words in automation
in the left then right speakers, reversing
while warning her audience, These are words
and not words that a person is speaking
and also no one, and always these words
are unreal. Synthesized. Children may hear
playtime, elderly hear *you die*, dieters
no pie. Rolling their heads from side to side
like insomniacs upon their pillows,
or a slow-mo drowning en masse, the crowd
teases different vowels and consonants
out of the warping madness. You will hear
what you deserve. Says the psychologist,
Let's try another. The War Reporter
whispers to the Poet, Anything yet?
Rainbow, replies the Poet. *Run away*,
smiles the War Reporter, *no brakes. Welcome*,
laughs the Poet, *love me. No way, no how,
nowhere,* thinks the War Reporter stumbling
over legs and feet and heads, desperate for
the exit. The audience is laughing
at the brain quirk. Parapsychologists,
this visiting British psychologist
jokes, tell me I've rediscovered a way
to hear the dead. But no one can tell me
why different people will hear different words
entirely.

The War Reporter Paul Watson Describes His Character

feeling like a dead guest on a talk show
couch with more dead guests and a dead host who
entertain a studio audience
of the dead, all for the invisible
dead who watch at home. *But sometimes at night*
he'll still dream of life. With so many friends
gone—what could be the reason? His penance
is reporting, but redemption will come
from dropping out, giving up, whenever
he finds the courage.

The War Reporter Paul Watson on the Really Real

My Chinese wife has some ancient wisdom
she'd like us to stick in our TV script
for bloggers in search of an Easter egg
in this Land of Illusion. *INT.*
— *dark hallway in Beirut,* reads the intro
to the character who's me, a haunted
yet handsome 50-something drudge cracking
the door on our Indian, hash-smoking
Buddhist therapist with a merciless
giggle and a few loose marbles. Karmic
about mental health, he doesn't believe
in Freud or SSRIs. And suicide's
so '90s. So he teaches acolytes
how to smoke the narghile pipe. Above
his rolling chair, gold characters dancing
balletically upon a battlefield
of silk incarnadine, the aforesaid
quotable which in loose translation reads:
The real is not real, just as the unreal
isn't really either.

The War Reporter Paul Watson Knows

The subject heading reads: *I know*. That name
mean anything to you? Didn't someone
once accuse you via email of not
asking for permission? from the family
of the dead, I mean, Dan. Speaking of which,
I'm happy to give you the Pulitzer
photograph. For your play. If the paper
protests, you can tell them I've given you
permission. Ha ha ha. As for other
pictures, are you looking for blood and guts
alone? Because I've got some guaranteed
to freeze you to the bone. I don't have one
with me in frame, I'm afraid. As you know
I'm superstitious. Chase after death and
death stops running. *Running beside runoff*
in the open culvert downhill, horses
and olive trees in pens. The local tongue
as birdsong. The Poet in Provence is
endeavoring to let the poetry speak
if it feels like it. While her belly swells
with Olivia, Ophelia, whichever
name she seems to ask for. The Judas trees
and epileptic cypresses, the shards
of ochre amidst cardinal poppies
like moths aquiver. The Times's Chivers
is where I ought to be. The West engaged
in self-soothing debates while mercenaries
penetrate the borders, tilting the board
in Assad's favor. Really makes me wish
I were your age, Dan, and childless. Two hands
for firing my Kalashnikov. Meet me
on the road to Damascus, if you catch
my drift. Ha ha ha. And another thing:

is our TV pitch likely to happen
this summer? I'll try to keep the hounds fed
till then. Before I go here's that email
I mentioned above, see if you can make
heads or tails of it. Or a poem. I know,
reads the subject. Followed by the message:
You will never be set free.

The War Reporter Paul Watson on the Link

I don't believe in ghosts that come rattling
to your bedside. Enmossed, enchained. Last night
my boy was begging me to sit with him
while he took his bath. But there's no such thing
as ghosts, I lied to him. Because truth is
I live with one. And I don't see him but
I'm forever feeling this need to feed
his hunger to be remembered. *Our link*
to killing has been broken, Dan. So we kill
too easily now. He did what he believed
was right at the time, shooting Somalis
from the sky. And I did what I believed
was right at the time, clicking my shutter
on his death. And in that instant our link
got fixed.

The War Reporter Paul Watson Rewinds the Film

Before this. My interpreter had asked
impatiently, Are you taking pictures
we can use? Is there film? Where is the light
coming from? Afraid to tear the unseen
sprockets, winding frame to frame. Forgive me,
I know I can get through this. It just takes
time. Because before this the mob had been
welcoming me to the banquet. Gamay
is here! my interpreter smiled. The Man
With Only One Hand. My reputation
unmanning me. My bodyguards leaping
out first. Because before this our driver
spotted the mob, towing death. Before this
I'd been sleeping on the hotel floor. Tires
on fire, vomiting smoke. Humvees strafing
the hotel's façade. Above the circle
that tied up the airport and the harbor
highways. Because before this I'd been just
one of the few who stayed behind after
Dan Eldon, Hos Maina, Anthony
—forgive me, I can get through this, I know
I will. Anthony Macharia and
Hansi Krauss. Four friends and reporters who
got beaten, stabbed, shot, stoned to a pulp. Some
castrated. As they scuttled to escape
a whirlpool of pulverized concrete as
the mob swept down. *Can they promise not to
kill us?* Because before this Black Hawks poured
cannon fire until that compound became
a cairn. For clan elders. All to abduct
the warlord Aideed. Tipped off before this,
he'd slipped away. While we'd been drinking beer
on the roof, admiring grenades like fleas

leaping under armored bellies before
bursting. Because before this men were taught
how to swap out the fuses for fuses
that detonate mid-air. They claimed they'd come
to quell the wailing with bread. Instead of
criticizing your own, the Pentagon
suggested, why not write about these ghost
-assassins? what are they calling themselves?
Al-Qaeda. Because before this soldiers
had been rappelling into mistaken
courtyards, grinding old men in pajamas
into the dirt, AK-47s
spearing the base of their skulls. This ballet
brut of aerial arrests. Mission creeping
like the traffic before this when a boy
in the back of a taxi smiled and slipped
the tip of his AK-47
through the window at me. As if to say,
Go home, American. Because before this
Mogadishu was pure. Villas washed white,
sands like brand new bandages. Forgive me,
forgive me, we'll get through this. It just takes
time.

The War Reporter Paul Watson on How to Eat Well

Enjoying a meal owes as much to fear
as to famine. Waking in the City
of the Dead, goose-stepping over corpses
coughing back to life. A man and woman
bathe a breathing skeleton with a bowl
of mud. Hips like sails. More corpses twisted
in sheets, lined up as trash. While the living
peer over the ledge, speechless. When the mob
opens its mouth: behold, a boy. His skull
like a crown. Passionate eyes devouring
me while I focus. It's frightfully clear:
eat or pass out. So I take five inside
this trattoria. A sanctuary
of fascist bric-a-brac. Hellfire boring
through bullet holes in stucco. Spaghetti
slung in terra cotta bowls. Two gunmen
level their barrels. Dollars, please. I kick
my camera beneath the table—fingers
snag the strap—a comical tug-of-war
until this skinny chef comes brawling through
swinging doors with machete poised, afraid
some dead white man would pose an obstacle
to profit. While the thieves laugh and flutter
into the world's oven. *When invited*
to cross the Green Line in Mogadishu
for beer and lobster with friends, happily
I found myself risking my life again
for a good meal.

The War Reporter Paul Watson and the Satellite Phone

I promised the Serbian concierge
I'd keep quiet. A bullet on a chain
nested in his chest hair. Rancid cologne
wafted across the front desk. Handing me
a can of warm Coke for my room. Alone
I reassembled the disassembled
pieces in the dark. Pristina closing
her eyes at night, as if NATO bombers
were Luftwaffe. Like a blind man fishing
for coils of wires inside my boots, circuits
foamy in my shaving kit. Nuts and bolts
balled up in my shorts. The plastic body
of the satphone layered in the folds of
pants, polos, pullovers. All together
the size of a brick. And the only place
to catch a signal was at the window
in the hall. With paramilitaries
patrolling the floors below, I skated
along the lino in my socks. Aiming
the miniature dish from the windowsill
towards low-earth orbit. Until the clunk
and whir of the elevator. The chain
cranking. Car clanking. Tenting hands to dowse
the screen's telltale glow. Smothering speakers
as the boot-up jingle brayed. Spastically
typing commands. As the elevator
juddered open, stayed open, his footsteps
slouching my way. My message flown, I slipped
past him like a notion, felt his warmth, ducked
into my room, easing the door, clutching
the knob, still, and holding my breath until
the elevator juddered closed again
and the door to his room shut. Then broke down

the satphone as before. Stroked the carpet
till my arm erupted in this tattoo
of hives, stashing the pieces in a tear
in the mattress. Just like I used to hide
my poetry, whenever as a boy
I dared speak my mind.

The War Reporter Paul Watson and the Dancing Boys

Birds fly with both wings when the Taliban
comes to town. But when the Taliban's gone
birds fly with one wing cause the other wing's
covering their assholes. The War Reporter
asks the Poet—Get it? Ancient Pashtun
Proverb! Because American soldiers tell
of farmers with kohl-blacked eyes, fingernails
oranged with henna, whinnying after
them in heels like newborn foals. Outside mosques
boys proposition: Like homo-sex? Quails
are their covert symbol. Like kite-fighting
and razors, too. Because they must be groomed
for love. For when a man finds his ashna
at the gym, say, a poster of Arnold
Schwarzenegger on the wall, he slips him
hashish, a wristwatch. A motorcycle
for the most adored. And almost always
wives and kids at home. While the baffled boy
rides shotgun. Dances with bells on his wrists
and ankles like Salome. *I like girls
but boys are easier. Because we never
see girls' faces. But we can always tell
which boy is most beautiful.* Every man
lets the Devil inside him, the cleric
squirms away. But AIDS is not a problem
here at least. Owing to isolation.
It is something we do and not something
we turn into. The ashna will grow up
to be husbands to the daughters of men
who rape them today. *Once upon a time
mujahedin fell in love with the same
beautiful boy.* In the conflagration
innocents perished. So Mullah Omar

unties their bells now. Chains them to stone walls,
then orders his bulldozers to topple
these walls upon them. As the Koran says
we must. *But they will crawl out of their holes
as soon as the Taliban go.* Bearded
faces towing spotless ones. When I ask
them a question, they shake their heads and fly
down the dirty road.

The War Reporter Paul Watson and the Son of the Tortured

She looks like a woman at first. A man
the same moment. A young father. Fetal
on the floral pallet, with another
floral bed beneath. Different flowers. Rug
seeded with ash. Head bound up and knotted
as if garlanded with ivy. To blot
out the memory, the wound. Throbbing upon
a turgid pillow, floral also. Spine
to the coral wall that reminds one of
the holy sepulcher. An empty bowl
in a niche, a plastic water bottle
half full of more swallows of tea. Could be
medicine. The torture victim's mute. Closed
eyes on an open fist, his own, cradling
a slack cheek. Collapsing, reviving. Sheets
swallow what's left of him, as if he's lost
his body. He breathes, we breathe. A boy sits
with muddy Wellies crossed. Kandahari
cap, geometric mirror flecks flashing
with his sneaking gaze, as he ascertains
not my camera but his father feigning
an endless sleep. Flies trace his sleeve. Our boy
decides. The doorway behind him plummets
deeper into evening.

The War Reporter Paul Watson and the Boys That Dragged the Body

Word got around: Bring the dead back to us
and you will be forgiven. *Sun setting*
on a squadron of barefoot boys hauling
one more. Blessed with dust. Rose holes. Uniform
shredding. Broken legs in a split. The boys
level their gazes at me through the glass
of the backseat. The smallest boy curling
his rope like a leash. Looped around the neck
of a man. Like me. *It's so difficult*
to describe, that scene. As a photograph
it would've been memorable. Believe me,
it would have won prizes! But people talk
of evil. I'm not a religious man,
never liked to use that word, but I saw
my own face photographed in their eyes. *Wind*
your window down, Paul. They want you to take
their picture. No thanks, I told the driver
—drive home.

The War Reporter Paul Watson on the Cliché

High-heeled shoe beside a puddle of blood
like Death's a lover and never a flood.

The War Reporter Paul Watson Takes a Stab

FADE IN — a paraffin lantern, relic
of the British misadventure, LISPING
like the tongue of the Deceiver. O/S
CALL TO PRAYER a reprieve. INT.
A BARN — PREDAWN PAUL, 50s, his hoarfrost
stubble BRUSHING dust out of a donkey
blanket. *Dan, you up?* You bet, boss. Bookworm
WRIGGLING for his contact lenses. *Let's go*
now, marines are pulling out, and Talibs
can't wait. Go knock on the farmhouse door for
—JOYCE, 20-something, Chinese, puffy lips
and tousled hair, shyly MOUSING her nose
over a stack of flour sacks, emblazoned
with the stars-and-stripes and Caucasian hand
-shake logo of USAID. Flies
PESTER her squinting eyes, as she NESTLES
another desert-infested blanket
to PERT NAKED BREASTS. *I burned my burqa*
last night at dusk, sneaking in here to sleep
beside—LAURENT, a Frenchman with a prick
-ish grin. This satyr ARCHING his bare back
behind his conquest. *We photographers*
have to, how do you Americans say? stick
together. Ha ha ha. Jesus, Joyce, (MORE)
if you don't want to see your tits FILLETED
and hanging from a tree, put some clothes on
and NOW! *Relax, I'll be out there shooting*
before you, old man. Gathering cameras
before panties. Dan packs his iPhone, Paul
can't find his pills. *LAURENT: Some combat-sex*
would sort that asshole out. EXT. — KEYS
TAPPING a scrap-wood door. Sunrise BARGING
in behind NAJIB, their driver: Go now,

sir. Time to leave. *We'll be ready, Najib,*
says Paul. Please thank our hosts for us, make sure
they've been paid enough. EXT. OUR GANG
TIPTOEING – MORNING to their Toyota
Land Cruiser. Fire-glazed, spider-webbed windshield
glass, zebra stripes of bullet holes. IDLING
in dung. *Sir, the farmer was angry.* Why,
Najib? *He said there is no guarantee
of safety now.* Then drive us to Kabul,
kemosabe. Then on to Starbuck's, QUIPS
our Frenchman. *Inshallah,* the driver STROKES
the blood-gold token of the Arabic
Dua-e-Safar, supplicant totem
for travellers, REVOLVING from the rearview
like air freshener, as the Cruiser DIVOTS
through this kind of medieval portcullis
CLATTERING down. *Najib, ease up a bit,
my dear?* Joyce SHOUTS. Najib appeals MUTELY
to the men who are ELSEWHERE, then slows down
a hair. *The farmer and his teenaged son
were sprawled at the side of the road. The man's
severed head rested on his shins. The throat
of the boy had been slit, blood like sun rays
soaked his stripped lean chest. Taliban with knives
watched us driving past.* Photographers SNAP,
reporter REMEMBERS, while the poet
SCHEMES. *Shukriya,* whispers Joyce. *Shukriya,
Najib,* which means thank you for some reason
in Hindi, I think.

The War Reporter Paul Watson on How YouTube

and Twitter work. The platforms. Kids come armed
with a smartphone, at least. Except their gaze
doesn't blink. A tripod, then. Monitoring
an alleyway in Homs from a warehouse
window maybe. Broken. Looted. Chatting
off-screen. Slurping tea. Yawning. Then this tank
trundles into frame like a Swiss cuckoo
clock or something, nose swiveling, boys shouting
Allahu akbar!—when anti-personnel
shells fry the frame with fireworks. Our rebels
can't speak, of course. But the picture remains
as it had been. Inviolate. Recording
that toy tank trundling away as YouTube
crossfades to a mosaic of thumbnails
to click on next. Imagine Confederate
soldiers bayoneted by their Union
brethren on touchscreens. Would we notice more
or less? Some food for thought. *Sent from my i*
-Phone to yours.

The War Reporter Paul Watson and the Arab Spring

In dead of winter Bouazizi wheels
his cart down the road. Outside a governor's
office in Tunisia. With his rotting
apples and oranges. Since he was ten
he fed his family. After his father's
heart infarcted in Libya, fitting stones
in Qaddafi's sprawling compounds. Speaking
of madness: Faida Hamdi, a woman
well into her 40s, sporting the dove
-blue uniform and matched, peaked cap, demands
the bribe Bouazizi never has. *Go*
home to your mother. Words become shoves and
Hamdi scatters Bouazizi's fruit and
Bouazizi may or may not punch her
left breast. She spits in his hair. His father's
a mongrel, she's a whore. Two policemen
sweep in and bludgeon and kick and stroll off
with Bouazizi's scales. He drags himself
into the governor's office, where a clerk
slaps him this time with words. Finding some fuel
somewhere, a friend or a construction site
nearby, it's unclear, he's back at the scene
of the insult. Dousing himself. Stinging
scrapes and bruises. Climbing into the bed
of his cart. Defiled. *How do you expect*
a man to live this lie? Flicks his lighter
till his pants catch fire. Panicking. Stumbling
in and out of his coat of flames. He falls
to his knees as traffic crawls. Fortunately
for democracy, people touch open
the cameras on their smartphones and enshrine
his performance. So many hands lifted
like fascist salutes are instead reaching

for an unobstructed view. One man's face is
slapped, and dictators' palaces topple
like trees that haven't borne fruit in years. Years
later in Beirut, sipping espresso
outside a café outfitted in pink
jasmine, my colleague replies, Why *should* I
risk my life? They're just going to upload it
to YouTube anyway.

The War Reporter Paul Watson and the King of Kings

Qaddafi. Self-anointed King of Kings
of Africa. Disguised as their brother
first, a David reading from his *Green Book*
of psalms. *Because men do not have the gift*
of childbirth, they do not suffer the strain
and stain of menstruation. Education
oppresses freedom. A baby's nursery
is his tyranny. And other such germs
of insanity. When flesh fell on hills
around Lockerbie, the Cowboy sent him
60 tons of revenge in minutes. Sun
-glasses thereafter. A face like Michael
Jackson. The circus tent. Wherein young girls
and boys got raped. The children of Libya
adore me! he would say. Why should I fear
my own children? *We are coming for you*
without mercy, the King of Kings promised
such rebellious children. But the children
of the Cowboy sent some drones from Vegas
to hound him into a highway drainpipe
plugged with shit. When his children pulled him back
into the sun weeping blood. His throat slashed
shallowly with a bayonet. Perhaps
a shot grazed his arm, or his breast. Perhaps
he got raped with his own golden gun. Slaps
rain down on the revealed, bald pate. Girlish
shrieking of men, frenzied yawping, shivering
for the thrill of justice. The golden gun
anoints his forehead. *Do you not recall*
what is right and what is wrong? Show mercy
for your father! He wears a Yankees cap
who blasts the back of Qaddafi's hollering
into a rosy echo. Old Fuzzhead

is dead, cries a father to his daughter
via cell phone. While the liberated
are playing with the King of King's body
like children with a hand puppet, gaping
then frowning the rank mouth as if he speaks
with their voice now.

The War Reporter Paul Watson and the Playboy

A troubled childhood, reads the leaked cable
from the Yankee diplomat. A caged room
in which his father would sic Rottweilers
on him. For misbehaving. So he'd fly
with schoolmates to Rome, Paris. Let's go there,
he'd say. No, let's go *there*. There was no way
he couldn't get the girl, and the boy too,
it must be said. Because he would make friends
watch porn with him, then demand they perform
oral sex, other things. Why not just *talk*
to her? they'd suggest—*that* will warm you up
correctly! His father married him off
to some general's fat daughter. Propped him up
at the head of a militia. As war
metastasized, the Splendid Gate afire,
he crossed the Sahara by Ferrari
to Niger. Secluded in a jungle
villa built by Libya. Watching women
barefoot on the sultry tar, balancing
plastic jugs of water on their heads. Worms
screwed in the mango. Dreaming of a life
in Mexico. And to think! once he'd lived
in his own villa. With his own caged room
in which he'd sic his own Rottweilers on
those who'd misbehaved. With cinder-block walls
around an al fresco disco, his pool
and cherished football pitch. Extradited
back to Tripoli, head and face shaved clean,
locked inside a caged room. Where he weeps still
for a father who paid Italian clubs
to let him suit up. And once in a while
even to play, slim legs swishing, handsome
opponents diving. Who would then gossip

after the match: If he were twice as good
as he is now, he'd still be twice as bad
as bad itself.

The War Reporter Paul Watson and the Dictator's Wife

She's pretty, still. When once she was the Rose
of the Desert, their Sunni Princess Di
or Antoinette, she's now the First Lady
of their Muslim idea of Hell, which is
a Women's Studies Course. Ha ha ha. Born
to an Acton heart surgeon, she required
her friends call her Emma. Then a BA
in Comp Sci and French Lit, the requisite
years investment banking. Anorexic
probably. A rechargeable battery
is what she calls herself. Married Bashar
somewhere in secret, bore him three children
so far. Two boys, a girl. Montessori
-educated. Who watch Harry Potter
movies on their MacBooks while she emails
Sotheby's for the price of a painting
of butterflies. In the meantime ordering
some Louboutin heels for seven thousand
USD. Doesn't wear a wedding ring
strangely, like the despot. Who emails her
this link to Nashville pop: *God gave me you
for the ups and downs / God gave me you for
the days of doubt.* While he's busy bombing
Homs, or making the calls. Charbroiled children
supine in the kitchen. Where teacups nest
pristinely on shelves. And in the next room
the smoking corpses of their parents spoon
beside the marriage bed. *God gave me you
for these days of doubt.* She goes on record
proclaiming, I will plant an olive tree
for every dead child! With her own children
filling new holes by hand. She has promised
never to leave: *I was here yesterday,
I'm here today, and I will still be here
tomorrow.*

The War Reporter Paul Watson and the Stones of Tahrir Square

Imagine David versus Goliath
-in-riot-gear. Tear gas and concussion
grenades. Cudgels, of course. A medieval
surge, foot by bleeding foot. Then bullets. Jets
taunting. Then opening wide the gates of jails
for murderers and rapists. Protestors
made shields out of cardboard and twine, twisted
railings for barricades, corrugated
tin like thunder sheets in the wind. Then stones
were harvested from craters. Even more
disinterred from garden walls. Citizens
traveled with their trowels. Leaving flowers
exposed as food for boots and sun. More stones
stolen from construction sites. Pockets, hand
-bags and suitcases full. As if prying
loose the stones would erase the fingerprints
of the hands that threw them! When eighteen days
had passed, Egyptians were replacing stones
wherever they found holes, and the country
had begun to look a lot like the old
country again.

The War Reporter Paul Watson Relaxes

Subject: for the drama. Dear Dan, sometimes
my flashbacks arrive like neatly stacked rhymes
in a bad poem. Barefoot in grass, gazing
from this mountainside towards a blazing
horizon, diastole-systole lurching
while NATO jets corkscrew skyward, searching
for their kill zone. Pinching myself, squinting
exhausted eyes. Where am I? Sick glinting
slivers slide like a fainting spell over
busted anti-aircraft batteries smoldering
behind the flowering berm. Fascinating
how quick. The so-called hallucination
familiar. The almost adoring call
of the murderous mob. *More to come, Paul.*

The War Reporter Paul Watson on the Meaning of the Absurd

It's July again so I've got corpses
on my mind. A friend tasked with shepherding
Dan Eldon's young body home. Other friends
lost that day. The liaison officer
says rules is rules and we can only move
bodies in regulation body bags.
Our friend fumes. The fan hisses. Everyone
knows how it feels to go to a funeral
for a friend, laid out there like she's not there
and yet she is, she fucking *was.* But how
can it feel to barter for hostages
in the blister of Bakara Market
when the ransom they want is so meager
that you know you've come too late? The perfume
in his Cobra T-shirt. Pure in the bed
of our galloping truck, the whip-smart cracks
of bullets, the boy singing, *Whenever*
I feel afraid, I hold my head erect
and whistle. Their bodies were recovered
from a trash heap in July. Now twenty
years ago today. That soldier remains
unswayed. Regulations. A man with heart
would've offered to clean them up before
their families would be collecting them from
that shimmering tarmac in Nairobi,
before Dan Eldon's burnt body would ash
ribboning through the limbs of acacias
rising up like ancestors from the tail
-end of Ngong Hills. Our friend asks how much
for four regulation body bags, then?
The officer enjoys this. We don't sell
our body bags. Ha ha ha. *Remind me*
to include this in our pitch, Dan, so that
executives in Hollywood can know
what I mean by the absurd.

The War Reporter Paul Watson Has the Time

Got an email from that interpreter
I helped escape from Kandahar. The dead
are Sayed's sister and sister-in-law
and the sisters' babies. Sayed's brother
Ahmed was the driver. To a funeral
in the desert. A bump in the road and
the usual dénouement. Dragging them
form the hemorrhaging, mangled carapace
into the brush. Where they bled out. One son
escaped with his father, leg like broken
bricks in a bag. Tubes draining wounds. *But where
is my mother? I want to sleep with her
again.* He tells his father: *Another
blast is coming. Why are we not going
someplace new?* Because the Taliban work
from meticulous lists. Like the ancient
Pashtun proverb says: You have the watches
but we have the time. I started to cry
when he answered the phone. *Everything, Paul,
is part of God's design. He will decide
who lives and who must die. But my family
are shopkeepers! students! I should have stayed
at home with them. Instead I ran away
from them.* The interpreter's family's blood
dried into black dust. Then helicopters
blew dust into the sun. We are the ones
to blame now. But I can't face the faces
of those whose mothers and babies are gone
because I was the one to post his name
online. Looking for wine, found this magnum
of champagne. Climbed in bed before midnight
last New Year's Eve, but not now. Suicide
gets bandied about with war veterans but

here's a novel idea: semi-retired
protagonist, pessimistic, packing
his pistol for protection, against all
sense and provocation, only to suck
it in his mouth and—blackout. The brother
of the interpreter got a phone call
this morning. *We will wait. For such people
as you, there can be no apology
or forgiveness.*

The Poet's Wife's Friend's Final Words

to the poet are disembodied. Sounds
like another hit! she texts. He marvels
at her apparent opinion. She greets
them in the corridor, blood burned off, skin
like grass under a stone. A memory
already, sojourning through a strata
of then and now at once. Her paper mask
unmasks her eyes. Her paper gown. Hearing
what's coming as she goes. They wash their hands
before embracing, the poet fearing
sickness—at this late stage! Everyone blames
Hoboken's leaching bricks. Laying kerchiefs
on her blanketed feet. He feels such shame
for when he found her nervous chatter hard
to bear, and told his wife so. He pities
her now. But what does he know? Of the ex
he'd always considered a prisoner
of conscience, somehow. The poet nurses
such resentment for every editor who
refused her. Who couldn't be bothered to
even reply. Though she'd been no worse off
than everyone. When his wife calls and says,
She's gone, the poet composes: *The day
isn't even half done.*

The Poet's Wife Dreams

In her casket she remains a patient
young woman, hands laced like contemplation,
fluids bruising her wrists. Her lips a seam
sewn crudely. Pursed, emptied first. In the dream
my wife's lively hands, darts which resemble
her mother's fine clay, as mine assemble
poems like my father turned screws, are turning
on the lamps in her childhood home, burning
grief out of the evening like a lover
prepares the scene. Only to discover
our friend here. Unstitching her mouth to cry,
You're not supposed to see me yet. She hides
behind the light. So when my wife lifts her
like a newborn to her breast to whisper
of our longing, she finds she's embracing
only herself, this wall she's facing.

What Really Scares the War Reporter Paul Watson

He's not afraid to die. Like Lazarus
unwinding his winding sheet in pursuit
of rebels in camos. Headbands with creeds
cross-stitched in Arabic. Rings on fingers
like Liberace. Pinging city streets
with Allahu akbar! before hammering
bullets around corners. *Sniper curtains*
rent asunder, we had to make a run
for our lives across the street. Hands on knees
in laughter in the alley. Laddering
into our own sniper's nest. *Boys are born*
to war, and men to die in them. Sharing
a bowl of milk tea by candle stub. Death's
almost like a friend, the war reporter
writes again. It's all this time spent waiting
around that just kills me.

The War Reporter Paul Watson on Wednesday's Chemical Weapons Attack

My editor attaches photographs
he says he can't publish. From the suburbs
of Damascus this morning. How I wish
I'd been there! to interpret this family
scattered like oracle bones on the tiles
of their kitchen. The dearth of furniture
is somewhat suspicious. A toddler's skin
turns, Father's chest bare, Mother spread-eagled
out-of-frame. Through the yawning window green
palm fronds and feathered ferns arrested mid
-breeze. Contemplating the crime, a stricken
man grimaces at our intrusion while
another's inhaling a sunbeam while
a third like a shadow blurs from the room
with hand to mouth. Or maybe he's smoking
a palliative cigarette. This picture
made me think hard. But my editor should
publish it anyway. And I plan on
telling him why.

The War Reporter Paul Watson and the Boys in a Crater

full of water. *Joy could be agony*
from a certain angle. Wet clothes sticking
to their bodies like cauls. Dead wires, bent pipes
dangling from the apartment block behind
sheared-off walls. Summertime in Aleppo
and the blue sky is breezy. Blue water
from a blasted main. Bright blue bicycle
parked in the rubble. *In an instant joy*
should be sorrow. One boy twists, his friend leaps
at us. Another boy in purple pants
considers, in danger of being knocked
flat by the lunger. One boy is rising
from his dip, football jersey wicking, hips
flexing as if surfing, pockets jam-packed
with something. Like what? Another boy's dropped
to his knees, collar of splashing water
almost regal around his neck, ulu
-lating with ecstasy, maybe. One slumps
on the lip of the crater, face in hands
as if collecting tears. *Their laughter is*
sorrow's best friend. I'm not in Syria
to take this picture, Freddie Paxton is,
but I can't tell you how happy I am
he's caught it.

The War Reporter Paul Watson on the Question of the Bombing of Syria

The before-shot's a Kurdish shepherd boy
leaning on his crook like a crutch. Gnarly
knob in his mouth like he's teething. With nails
chewed ragged, crescents of grime. A snowflake
pattern knitted in a Christmas sweater
with sleeves unraveling. Polyester
slacks, one presumes sneakers. Donated by
Cheney and Bush. His name might even be
Cheney or Bush, a common tribute. Dust
coats his dusky face. Gazing dreamily
back behind my camera. Behind his back
his family's out-of-focus flock grazes
between flat rocks. Horizon as if steeled
for what's next. *The after-shot's just the flock*
scattered and sprawled like suitcases after
an airliner's blown out of the sky. Scorched
wool billowing in the breeze. Sheep are prone,
their penises pointing. Blood like jam clots
every orifice. Freewheeling vultures
have pecked out eyes, tongues. And nobody knows
where the shepherd boy has gone. Peshmerga
barking like a showman, Kalashnikov
slung over his shoulder, mustached and fat
like a bureaucrat. *If the US has*
such smart bombs, why can't they tell the difference
between enemies and sheep?

The War Reporter Paul Watson and the Room across the Hall

It's like they're still in college. Mattresses
on the floor. Empty soda bottles filled
with water. Chicken bones and French fry stubs
in clamshell cardboard. Toilet rolls along
electric radiators. One laptop
like a fire in the cave mouth at night. Cords
suckling at working sockets. A tissue
box for unmentionables. Mugs and Moleskine
diaries. Backpacks, blankets. A feather
duster in a pressure cooker. Kevlar
vests and helmets, bullets, Kalashnikovs
and concussion grenades. I caught a glimpse
whenever they came or went. Jawboning
behind their door like they were debating
the death of God or Freud. And once I heard
English barked in a Brooklyn accent but
covered my ears for fear. Spat my toothpaste
into a kidney dish. Sank to my couch
cushion on the floor. In my solitary
room across the hall. Kevlar vest, camera
in my helmet. A pillar of sunrise
through Venetian blinds. While the muezzin
rouses Aleppo: *Hurry to prayer,*
hurry to success! They dragged a mattress
through my door, loaded with a newish corpse,
or so I thought at first. Black hair like moss
growing over a bullet scar. Breathing
miraculously. His midnight tracksuit
with Adidas stripes. Sharp cheeks, hennaed beard
sculpted handsomely by his friends. Bare feet
smelling of urine. While they were mopping
their room across the hall, the living corpse
watched me. As if smiling. As if sharing
his faith: *Hurry to prayer, hurry to*
success!

The War Photographer Lynsey Addario Tells
the War Reporter Paul Watson

On the road to Aleppo, while long-range
missiles spark overhead with sarin gas
for children. Women. You can imagine
the emotions! And here she comes crawling
back from the border. We're just chatting like
you do, you know, dirty jokes and horror
stories over cocktails. When she tells me
something I don't know: how she's grown used to
being touched. In public. In Tahrir Square
and more so-called official venues where
she's just waiting for some dignitary
to scissor his ribbon: she's a woman
in a press of men. And every man feels
they can. *Dragged out of her golden sedan*
by loyalists. Her driver Mohamed
raises his hand to the vomiting hole
in his heart. She's bashed in the face. Whiplashed
into the street. Blindfolded. Hands and feet
winched behind her back with her own laces.
Steve confessed later the bayonet's pressed
into his anus. His linen trousers
tore. She's lucky, she tells me. *Every man*
who lifts me to move me is feeling my
tits, pussy. I wear a hijab, I know
enough not to kick and shout. I perform
the Muslim porno: *I have a husband*
like you. Please don't. Please don't. In the belly
of a tank now. He cups my mouth, whispers,
Don't speak. Please don't. Please don't. Then spooning me
as if heartsick. Untangling my hair
with tears in his voice, he croons, *You will die*

tonight. But remember Steve who got poked
with that bayonet? ask and he'll tell you
—Better than a bullet! So don't you see
what I'm after here? I don't want to sound
like O the poor woman. Because it was
a shame, but at the same time it's crucial
we're honest. *I change the subject.* She's scared
to go anywhere now, she dips her toe
into the acid bath. Hoping to feel
a reason again. I'm willing to talk
to counselors, she says. But I won't talk
to anybody who can't understand
what it's like to be a woman at war.

The War Reporter Paul Watson on Machismo

Ex-military are the worst. Breakfast
at a Novotel in Turkey en route
to the border. With CIA fumbling
tongs at the hot bar like they've been handling
gun shipments to rebels. When she flags me
over. *Is that you?* My tray in my hands
like a crater-face in some Hollywood
high school. And the guy she's with's a muscle
-bound Belfastard. Thousand-yard glare. Tipsy
with testosterone from the front coursing
through his veins. Looking at me like, Who's this
fecking eejit? So I sit down and I begin
to namedrop where I've been, while he namedrops
the caliber of the handgun he keeps
in his Y-fronts. No longer performing
the age-old journalistic pantomime
of acting like we're innocent, even
when we know we've never been.

The War Reporter Paul Watson Prefigures the End

Have you thought about it? You should. Watch it
on your computer. You won't be the same
after, or you will be and that will be
your problem. If I were you, Dan, I'd cling
to life. Most everyone should. Your unborn
child deserves the splendid world. But your fear
is what you failed to mention: your own eyes
rolling in her mother's face. A table
between you in Carmel-by-the-sea. Blessed
with the air of a classicist. Copper
-colored curls. Determined. Passionately
decoding your codex. And what have you
become? a ghost? *As they're laying the knife
against your throat.* Will you thank them? I will
giggle like Gandhi. Slyly, perverted
with pride, they'll presume. I'll forgive them when
they slice my skin, snap sinews and larynx
and gullet and spine, carotid arteries
spraying like pinched hoses while I'm drowning
in a gibberish calling for this cup
to pass my lips. I won't believe it and
neither should you, my friend. As they string me
up like some Biblical scapegoat and O
never mind the details. I will have gone
into the dangling bulb and sinking sun
in this land where all the trouble began,
the Cradle, don't they call it? the Cradle
of Man.

The War Reporter Paul Watson Dreams of Poetry

Last night I dreamed Syrian kidnappers
shot a video for YouTube of me
beaten with hoses. Water-boarded. Mock
-executed. *Who I give this gift to?*
he seethes. *Who I give this gift to?* He fires
into the ceiling and plaster pummels
my head. So he gives me some juice. Scripting
my pleas to pressure the paper to pay
my ransom. Because Hezbollah Shiites
know in their bones how poetry changes
hearts and minds, they provide some Persian verse
that magically I comprehend. *Your heart
and mine are holding hands.* Pure Islamic
pederasty, if you ask me. But soon
they're handing me a pen and paper and
demanding I write and read aloud and
I'm delighted to find I can reveal
who I am, how I feel, how I am here
by a well, near a camel, in a code
of iamb, trochee, spondee. Allusions
in my poems to other poems have become
life and death, finally. For critics in
Alexandria to triangulate
my captivity. Navy SEALs flopping
out of the bellies of gunships with night
-vision goggles, laser-crosshatched bullets
blasting to bits the astonished foreheads
of our literary foes. I don't know
much about poems, but what do you think, Dan,
could it work?

The War Reporter Paul Watson Has Some Dialogue
For Future Use

Al-Nusra in the ruins doesn't care
to have his picture taken. He could have
simply stepped aside: a severed doll's head
sipping from a puddle. Why are you here?
the rebel's probably saying in a tongue
of concrete dust and vomit. In a tongue
of whiskey I reply: *You do your job,*
killer, and I'll do mine. During dinner
we discuss the clip of another head
of another soldier buried in dirt
up to his chin, deliriously gulping
for air. As a spade slowly baptizes
him with showers of more dirt. Then black boots
tamp down his cries. A German filmmaker
gulps his macchiato. You are travelling
with rebels, Paul! You must remain neutral:
rebels also commit war crimes. Look, Hans,
I reply, I'm all for the rounding up
and shooting. *It's the burying alive*
I can't stomach. This reporter's writing
her memoirs. Her parents were hairdressers,
her dad, surprise, was gay. Her sister wrote
Parent Trap, uncredited, and a script
inspired by her sister's PTSD
that died on the shelf when the studio head
got scalped. I say, I need someone like you
in my TV show! And she laughs, *Only*
if you promise to let me live.

The War Reporter Paul Watson Dreams of Freedom

Here's a JPEG of the boat I've christened
Uhuru I, Uhuru II being
40 feet long, with a gourmand's galley,
hot-water head and a beehive of beds
stowed below. But Uhuru I is all
I can afford now, this dingy dinghy
like scum in a flashflood. Benching in time
to slip another howler, which I'll take
as a good sign. Huddling in the cabin
built with my one hand. Electricity's
in our future, with any luck. Water
sings leaping from the squeaking wheel. Ocean
-grit grinding clean a salvaged floor. Fire pit
downhill from a door I'll sometimes secure
with a combo lock. Seems like every time
I'm here it rains. But I'll bring you with me
when we sell our TV pitch. We will write
beneath the pines, drinking exclusively
Canadian Cabernet. And we'll have sailed
Uhuru II, which translates as freedom
in Swahili, by the way. Tomorrow
I'll be home. In the hands of a new wind
I still have hope.

The Poet Confesses

We love war, your mother and I adore
our Shakespearean meltdowns. She will assault
your father's frail ego, and he'll go all
Lear on himself. Feels good. Then rain the tears
upon the howling heath. But who doesn't
need a good war? In Kabul, Aleppo.
Chicago, LA, DC—we envy
the dead! Why else would we send so many
thither? and just as zestily stir up
reinforcements. Who come crying hither,
quoth the poet. And go guttering from
the tall tallows of their lives. *With curtains*
wavering in windows, palm fronds dashing
themselves to the street like cranes committing
suicide. Shy Mercedeses. And crows
darting across the sky. The light is all
there is to notice the seasons curling
into or out of the dust. While the muse
uses me, just as you spend your mother's
summer body. Here's to hoping you come
hither bawling and wawling. *Delivered*
from the womb into the womb of the world,
from the world into words. Every father
should beg for forgiveness, first. If this life
be some mysterious school, or some other
New Age nonsense. I fear it is nothing
but blood pooling on the tiles like a shout
cooling in a thought above the corpse of
Cordelia in the food court of that mall
in Nairobi today. I'm blind. I pray
you do not cast the shadow of my grief
when first you breathe and cry upon this stage
of lies. I forgive your mother, and she
has forgiven me. I prithee. Mark me,
my child.

The War Reporter Paul Watson on the Death of Mandela

Everyone fights civil wars. Mandela
surprised us all, coming to the table
early. His trademarked searchlight smile sweeping
away my gloom. Engulfing my white hand
in his boxer's paw. He spoke of struggle
academically. Said he was just one
of many, after 27 years
surviving solitary. Whites killed blacks
yesterday with a pipe bomb blotting out
a township restaurant. Then a hundred
kilo bomb greased a taxi stand teeming
with blacks queuing for their daily commutes
into town. So blacks pulled whites from their sky
-blue Mercedes. Who do you think you are?
and worse yet, What do you think you're doing
in our country? Then head shots. *We are here*
to heal old wounds. Even Afrikaners
are friends now. Even Terre'Blanche, white poet
prancing on his black horse? Hemingway's beard
and Göring's baby blues. Shoveling fascist
bullshit to shitheads with swastikas scrawled
on armbands and flags. Terre'Blanche beat a black
man in a park once, sicced his dog on him
for testifying against a white. Jail
-time followed, surprisingly. *Till he's found*
in bed on his farm years from then, spatter
like a Jackson Pollock. Hatchet job. Pants
around his ankles. Used condoms littering
the scene. Two black farmhands, one still a boy,
claiming he'd raped them. The older killer
considered castrating Terre'Blanche before
he lost the nerve. *While the poet's black horse*
ran riderless in its pen. Invite them

to this table, knocked Mandela. Hatred
is a thought that bursts into blows when stopped
from speaking. *Took a train to Zululand*
to have tea with Buthelezi. Who'd mocked
Nelson the house slave. I quoted de Klerk
on Buthelezi allying himself
with scumbags like Terre'Blanche—*If you want this*
interview to end! Upright and clinking
his cup to his saucer. Buthelezi,
who claimed to be the blood inheritor
of Shaka Zulu, conceived of power
as his birthright. Whereas Mandela, prince
of the Xhosa tribe, proclaimed that power
is the people's. *Mandela is dying*
in Johannesburg. Finally. Breathing
by the grace of machines. We have kept him
with us too long, selfishly. Reporters
have this way of letting editors know
a story's done: no space all caps three times
ENDIT ENDIT ENDIT.

Now The War Reporter Paul Watson Really Sounds Old

Your poetry is elevating you
to a nobler calling, curator to
my memory museum. Serving a tour
of duty in southwestern Ontario,
I dropped some white lightning on a picnic
and thereby bungled my one-and-only
chance to romance a receptionist with huge
owlish spectacles that were all the rage
in the '80s. Sublime breasts too, or so
I remember hoping. Things got swirly
before she bolted into the Van Gogh
of those schizo tobacco fields. To file
your story, you'd have to slip in between
the ropes with this Teletype machine
whose keys would punch back, then jam if you stopped
stroking like a butterfly. To be sure
your copy had landed you'd type ENDIT
no space all caps three times. I was typing
well into the '90s on one of those
black-and-green Tandy screens that interfaced
with the proto-web via cumbersome
rubber couplers. Whispery phone lines snapping
over No Man's Land. I'd sit up at night
watching every word of my story scroll
slowly left to right, smoking a spliff while
telling myself there's no nobler calling
than wasting one's life for a so-called truth
some junior editor might or might not
scrape out of the bowels of the mainframe
at One Yonge Street. Now I really sound old.
But I remember when. And I miss it.
And that's not nostalgia. ENDIT ENDIT
ENDIT indeed.

The War Reporter Paul Watson Shovels Shit

Funny you should mention it. I'm tempted
to send you the file of my failed attempt
to pump this bouncer at The Foggy Dew
in Coquitlam: Did you see the mayor
slip into the staff washroom? pursued by
unnamed associates, only to fall
out like an hour later and I'm quoting,
speaking in tongues and frothing at the mouth
and nose and twitchily rhapsodizing
just intelligibly enough to hoist
another round of beers, rum-and-Cokes, shots
of JD's. And other chestnuts floating
round the web. Go ahead and Google me
and you'll see, I told him, by which I meant
the Pulitzer. See, G. Gordon Liddy
once proved his trustworthiness to a mole
by placing the palm of his hand over
the flame of his Zippo, until the flesh
cooked. But as you know, Dan, I've only got
the one hand, ha ha ha, and I don't smoke
cigarettes, at least. America is great
because you all want fame, but Canadians
prefer politeness. And this bartendress
is a nurse, according to her Facebook
page at least. So here I am staking out
her hospital in search of some buxom
trailer-trash type, trying hard not to look
too skeevy. I wish I knew how to write
what people want to read. Then all this shit
might be worth something. Now, to my Friday
bottle of wine.

The War Reporter Paul Watson on the Silent Apocalypse

You can literally watch it happening
in newsrooms all around the world: where once
there'd been like these feeding frenzies of men
in vast, cacophonous pens, now you see
coffee-stained carpets and huddled masses
of mourners wishing farewells to colleagues
quitting or fired, amidst the grunts squealing
desks on dollies towards elevators,
and what was once Empyrean has been razed
like some mud-bricked bazaar in Pakistan,
where toothless grandmothers duck and cover
children from the circling drones. Gone are shouts
of, you know—Stop the presses! and all that
golden-age lingo dwindling to ticking
fingers on smartphones. *Cluelessly searching*
for scissors my first day, someone pointed:
Copy desk, Einstein. Where they'd been soldered
to a chain. So I asked the copy boy,
Do journalists steal them? No, journalists
stab each other in the neck, ha ha ha.
Is that funny, Dan? Or sad. All I know
is that lately I've been missing our kind
of dedication.

The War Reporter Paul Watson on How Times Change

Remember necklacing in the townships
where they'd grab a white guy and slam a tire
full of petrol over his head and arms
and set him on fire? Under apartheid
you'd think I'd be just the person to give
that necklace to. But they were like, You're free
to observe. *When another tire blows out
in Helmand Province.* My fixer's chatting
inscrutably with a mechanic while
I burn in the sun. On the road again
he says: That mechanic was suggesting
we saw your head off and offer it to
the Haqqanis. Fifty-fifty. *And what
did you say?* My car is clean. Ask me when
my car is already dirty—ha ha
ha!

The War Reporter Paul Watson Accuses the Poet

Good news about the sporadic interest
in your poems. But you'll have to retitle
this embryonic opus *The Former
War Reporter*. Because I can't persuade
bosses to send me back to Syria
or even Kandahar. I keep chipping
away, but all they do is look past me
with eyes darting, as if half-expecting
Sirhan Sirhan. I don't know why, maybe
it's the insurance. Because this latest
hitch concerns so-called accidents. I asked,
Are death by crossfire and execution
both covered? No response yet. It's a cost
-benefit thing: Why do we need to go
now? And if we *do* go now how will we
find the extra hundred thousand dollars
needed to retrieve the beheaded corpse
of Watson? Given current financial
bellwethers. It's like trying to reason
one's way off of Death Row. Not long ago
bosses were fond of treacly platitudes
about The Need To Bear Witness. Bullshit
then, bullshit now. But excellent training
for Hollywood, right? Though do I wonder
if your poems are to blame. Because bosses
should never know you're human. Even though
I'm sure editors don't know how to read
poems. Ha ha ha. Which is why I'm spending
all my free time attempting a hobby,
mycology. It's taking much longer
than expected: misting, fanning, sniffing
assiduously. When you come visit me
on my island to write our TV script

together in my cabin, we'll trip balls
for inspiration. Then take a long hike
out past Murder Point. Where the First Nations
peoples threw off their colonial yoke,
for a time.

The War Reporter Paul Watson after Aidan Hartley

Why don't you plagiarize somebody else
for a spell? Once upon a time wizards
hammered an obsession into the tree
of my mind. Via photograph. Implies
Watson in retelling Hartley's feature
quoting Gerald Hanley's classic memoir
of Somalia called *Warriors: the whirling*
sand and demonic heat amidst furies
of flies. Calling from dunes like bloodied hands
around the chalice of the sea. White mosques
as if sketched by pre-Raphaelites, the light
-house beams spanning Djibouti to Rome, light
-skinned iterations of slave traders. Poems
in Swahili. Sandalwood pheromones
and halwa meats sweetening the sandy streets
of Barawe. So unlike the carcass
of Mogadishu, where the wind still flutes
through ruins like reefs. *I swam and I slept*
in a mansion, writes Hartley, canjeero
baking in the yard below. Hoisted up
to me with lamb's liver, sesame oil
on oval copper trays, pulleys peeling
a coconut rope. Why didn't I stay?
learn Chimbalazi, fish for yellowfin,
purchase a deed from elders in the Isle
of Dogs, or Minneapolis. *I walked*
into the sun instead, a man bewitched
by his dream of truth. SEAL Team 6 launches
another midnight raid, slinking away
with the sinking tide, while the sons of God
whet their father's knives, then slice out the tongues
of the innocents of Barawe.

The War Reporter Paul Watson Salvages the *Terror*

Never play poker with underwater
explorers, who'd later describe their mood
as sphincter-tightening. Swabbing the deck
of all talk of their mission whenever
I'd show up. On this icebreaker surfing
the internet can be a pain, even
on a good day, but the helmsman merely
shrugged and suggested we'd been vectoring
through satellite shadow. So back down, Paul,
to hurl in your hammock, watching the wheel
of death on your laptop spin. *A chopper*
pilot patrolling the flinty margin
of Queen Maude's Gulf, in his neon-orange
drysuit, red-tasseled toque, shotgun balanced
on his shoulder, shepherding scientists
past polar bears. Espies a winking bit
of iron winch, rusted, shaped like the head
of a tuning fork, stamped with the logo
of the Royal Navy. *So we deploy*
our arsenal, robot subs and multi
-beam 3D sonar towfishes, sidescan
relics just in case, a silver bullet
-nosed beauty with jet-black fins delivering
that Eureka! moment. When the Falcon
turns its dread eye on the wreck. *Lord Franklin*
was bald and stout with mutton chops, dreaming
of the hidden passage. But as they sing,
No man may know. *Until the Esquimaux*
in their skin canoes saw ghost ships encased
in floating floes, like a Viking funeral
after the pyre's blown out. A bald and stout
man with mutton chops below, skin like bronze
statuary, eyes like split marble, teeth

like walrus tusks because one's gums will shrink
into the scurvy smile. *Chilling to see*
shimmering in the amniotic green
of the monitor, her body intact
save for three masts sawed off by ice shearing
in geological time, missing planks
like black keys, mossed cannonry, furred debris
scattered. Slurries of seaweed. Cold water
preserving all. *But is she* Erebus
born of Chaos into eternal night,
or Terror? my personal favorite. And where
is her sister then? Closer to the point
of abandonment, the historians
would have you believe. But who knows? Someone
scrawled farewell in a note, sealed it inside
one of those poisonous meat cans, soldered
with leaching lead. Buried three of their dead
in the permafrost, where even today
their corpses thrive, lustrous locks flowering
around mummified, scurvy smiles. Ghastly
male undines. After a hundred souls heaved
the drag-ropes of their lifeboats on sledges
across snow like sand, ever south into
the brim of sun, losing their minds, carving
comrades out of tin kettles—well you know
the old song. No tongue should tell. An ancient
mariner sums it up well: *The* Terror
was just waiting to be found.

The War Reporter and the Poet Share a Curse

Why do I write back to you? Why do you
write to me? Why not lay our weary heads
upon our arms and weep? How can you think
we're the same? when everything's been going
your way, relatively. *When my family
turned their backs on me, Paul, they were asking,
Where have you gone? And with the spring the snow
gives up the trash of fall.* Praise be the green
caulking up sidewalk cracks. Heap praise on dirt
for your unborn child's sake, if no other
reason. *But can't you tell me the reason
you're still here, Paul?* I lie to everyone
save my wife and son. I shrink from the truth
now more than ever. A bottle of wine
on a Friday night, something I suspect
has become daily for you. *To admit
I mourn them is to say I miss the hate
they engendered. Or should I say I mourn
a peace not yet achieved?* Why do we write
still? You won't let me go, and I believe
I don't deserve to be.

The War Reporter Paul Watson's Fear of Los Angeles

Rising up through the earth, elevator
opens in Perfumes. Trial makeovers
for reptilian starlets. So many puffed
-up lips, surprised eyelids. Can't stop screaming
in the dream. *So I've been searching for flights
and wondering,* Why don't I stick around
till Monday for postmortem? We will sell
this pitch, or we won't. And if nothing else
there's always Disneyland. Is the subway
worthwhile? Because once I made a wrong turn
out of LAX and I found myself
back in Mogadishu. Corpse collectors
shoveling flesh like cinders, flashing their death
-glares at me through the splintering windshield. Death
-glares while beating the dead American. Teeth
scarred by qat chewed to sharpen their hacking
skills. Every white man is a murderer,
they think, with reason. *I hung a U-turn
across Sepulveda, I think it's called,
with two African-Americans speeding
down on me.* Their Lincoln SUV. Death
-glare from the passenger seat, his finger
pointing as they passed. His thumb cocked. His Glock
just out of reach, in the glove compartment,
one presumes.

The War Reporter Paul Watson Will Be Staying at the Holiday Inn

by the airport. In the past the grinding
in the pit of my stomach was for fear
of dying. Now I'm scared of coming home
to the same life. Ha ha ha. *Difficult Men:*
Behind the Scenes of a Revolution
in TV on my tablet. From Tony
Soprano to Walter White. Psychopaths
speaking for our psychotic times. It's fun
to envision our future creations
killing each other, themselves. I'm convinced
we're the legitimate heirs to the throne
of critically adored and sadistic
TV for grownups. Grandiosity's
my métier. And you can authenticate
our dialogue, right? No matter what happens
in Hollywood we'll have a few stories
to raise the grandchildren by. I'm happy
to be alive, Dan! like I haven't been
since Desert Storm One. A revolution
in faith: that the imagination can
lift one out of this post-traumatic slough
of boredom. See you tomorrow, tonight
I'll be strolling down Airport Blvd.
in search of a McDonald's.

The War Reporter Paul Watson on the Smell of Fear

Thankfully it's rare. Your body weeping
out of every pore. Armpits, crotch. Your neck's
instantly slick, singing. Amygdalas
of bystanders go nuts! contagiously
like yawning. Like death. Not the smell of death
per se, but of the body spending life
to live. But often fear's in vain. A shame
-ful reek inside your mother's hat. Father's
milky condom in the trash. Worse than milk
gone bad. Or feces, urine. Genitals
unwashed, menstruating. Typically fear leads
to procreation. If smell could be seen
fear would be less fearsome. Do you know why
officers prefer khaki? quoth the wag.
To better hide the stain, though every soul
born smells it.

The War Reporter Paul Watson's Obsession With Combat Sex

War is hot, embedded or not. War strips
myelin from ganglions. Naked breathing
across the tarmac, strafing pursuing
me like suitors. Whenever I was scared,
writes the poet, my father would soothe me
with, Relax, you'll never hear the bullet
that blows your brain apart. This from a man
who never served. *Somewhere in Kosovo*
the walls of the safe house were rocking like
a honeymoon suite. With NATO bombing
us back to the Stone Age. We snaked Ritalin
out of their gelatin capsules, milling
molecules free of their time release. Souls
coupling and tripling while I sat longing
for my wife back home. My only son born
within the year. *While the poet's hand rests*
upon his wife's womb. Feeling the flicker
of a future like thunder or mortar
approaching. So when we combine it all,
the boredom, the fear, the stench of bodies
you've shot that day, your first inclination
isn't to fuck. You would think. But it's like
those spikes in population in the wake
of hurricanes, earthquakes, and other forms
of rapture? the poet adds. That's right,
replies the war reporter, as if shocked
he's not speaking to himself.

The War Reporter Paul Watson and the War Tourists

This Japanese guy walks into a bar
in Beirut. Could be Amman. Some tubby
trucker from Hiroshima. Commuting
back and forth to Syria. Tiger-stripe
camos, Keffiyeh, telephoto lens
like an albatross. Video camera,
Toshiba of course. Boots. Without thinking
he needs a vest or helmet, he's acting
like a kind of Hollywood avatar
of who I am. What we do. Like Disney
has a ride called Aleppo! He's just one
of a lost tribe. With no real intention
of selling his pictures of an IS
fighter with legs blown away, gesturing
calmly like, Some help here please? Or this mom
knelt like she's praying on her son, a hump
in the pavement, brilliant blood blaring through
overexposed sheets. You can see this and
more on his Facebook page. Fukushima's
the name, or it should be, at least. Living
the dream, he says. Divorced, he hasn't seen
his daughters in years. *I bought insurance*
so every day in case I'm killed my girls
will at least make money. This character
is somebody familiar. Yet I feel
superstitious. Chase after death and death
stops running—remember? What time's our pitch
at Showtime, Dan? We're going to need a bite
to eat first.

The War Reporter Paul Watson on the Devourer of Hearts

He opens the body in a crater
of earth and rubble. With dirt the color
of menstrual blood. Hacking like a husband
barbecuing. Gouging a fish's mouth
into the pallid breast, through which he plucks
a heart and lays it on a plank across
the corpse's solar plexus. You're carving
him a Valentine! laughs the cameraman
perhaps. Embarrassed birdsong, light shredding
of human meat. Gristle-flicking. He lifts
the heart with knife in hand. The other hand
scoops up a hunk of lung. We will devour
your hearts and livers, you mercenaries
of Bashar the Dog! Then ritually chews
into flesh that breathed. Not heart, or liver
as reported. The video seizes
with that bite like a kiss. Allahu akbar!
voices had been shouting. *God is greater
than whom? we'd do well to ask.* Just a man
from Homs, who before the Spring sold lamb's meat
in the streets. Teased olive branches beneath
the noses of Bashar's dogs. A woman
and child chanting—two shots, his brother stooped
to help—through the neck, he bled out next. More
friends and a lover lost. The police called
him on his cell so he could feel the sound
of his parents beaten. And remember
that loyalist carried a video
in his phone: girls made to watch their mother
raped with sticks. When their turns came. Then all stabbed
as if clinically. You weren't bothered
by any of that—why not? Picture yourself
in my shoes, he says. Like I told the ghost

of that American soldier years ago
in Mogadishu: *I didn't want to
do this, I had to do this.* It is true
I have changed. I have become the Angel
of Death, he says. Here to devour the hearts
of men like beasts.

The War Reporter Paul Watson Outside the Medical School in Aleppo

Sebastian stripped of flesh: his skeleton
in a trash can. Students smoking. His jaw
dangling from a hinge. His cranium worn
like a yarmulke, or a plate spinning
on a shining rod that shepherds the spine
down into floating hips. The crucifix
of sternum and clavicles, bowed ribs sprung
as if phantasmal lungs within still heave
for passion, escape. This tool for teaching
got busted in last night's bombing. Thrown out
to make way for skeletons imprisoned
in mortifying flesh. Look closely and
you'll notice: behind the spine is the spine
of a sapling tree. And this trash can's not
what it appears to be, but an old pot
for sapling trees. Which only proves the rule
that students of medicine everywhere
must have a sense of humor.

The War Reporter Paul Watson at the Courthouse/Jail

Our last hope for peace will come from lawyers
and judges in this apartment complex
-cum-courthouse/jail. Where shell blasts trouble
bones and windows. Assault rifles rankle
like a street festival. We're listening
to a policemen gripe about these ghost
-militias sucking blood from businesses
like America used to. Our millionaires
fled into Egypt, the shame of the rich
of Syria! he cries. The judge fumbles
for middle ground. Men of God will decide
with their hearts, he philosophizes, bulbs
stuttering, paint flaking. *But men of law
have no such luxury.* While below us
ghost-militias entangle like orgies
out of Bosch, on wall-to-wall carpet, sick
generator spitting. Lake of leaking
rainwater encroaching. The jailor's light
stirs the flesh. Razor spines as if threatening
to tear through skin. A fundamentalist
rebel admitting to raping two girls
smiles through the bars. The jailor says, He'll live
until we receive a mandate from all
the people. To do otherwise would be
a crime as well.

The War Reporter Paul Watson in a Coffee Shop in Aleppo

Every revolution has a problem
with power. Submitting Afghanistan
as an example: jihadis will come
with strings attached. Beheadings and stonings
and young girls raped in the name of marriage
—the works! Surely you have not risen up
against millennia of tyranny
only to pimp your kids for these psychos
instead? A young man rises. Your country
did nothing. Pointing, crying. I wonder
if he could hit me. Have I betrayed him
personally? Trying to smooth things over,
an old man interjects: We do not love
jihadis. But the more our people die
the more we *learn* to love.

The War Reporter Paul Watson amidst the Generations

A young man is signaling an old man
to slow down and stop. The old man's nosing
a motorbike through rubble with a boy
in his lap. Wheat-colored hair marks the boy
the scion of Templars. While our young man's
Al-Nusra, desert-skinned. The old man grins
like Arafat. The boy wears a sweatshirt
that reads bluntly—Gap—his knuckles dimpling
as he gingerly accepts the assault
rifle from our rebel. *Who had earlier*
unbuttoned his shirt to display these scars
like pink planets curving from his belly
to his breast. Take the shot now. With his breath
peeling in veils. Sloe-eyed. One bullet sleeps
beside his heart, he says. Told the surgeon,
Leave it for Allah and let me go back
to war. *Our boy is giggling like a boy*
throwing back the sash. His slender fingers
tickling the trigger. The rebel's pinching
the muzzle into a sullen sky while
his free fingers resemble a peace sign
by mistake, most likely. The old man's smile
betrays its opposite. Take the shot now,
repeats the rebel. *Afterwards he'll rip*
a banana-clip from his vest to prove
the gun wasn't even loaded. Tell me
what your tattoos mean? as I trail behind
like a cur in the street. This one's a poem
to my brother. He coughs. Assad removed
his penis. But first his fingers. Beat him
with pipes, shocked him with wires. Starved him until
he was just this wisp of smoke to be cut
with the waving of a hand. Dumped inside

a hole with rats, melting snow. *Can you tell
me what this tattoo means?* There is no more
family, it reads. No more brothers. Beware
especially the friends who are friendliest
to you. Smiling as he hands me his flask
of water. Take, drink, I am not the same
man as the man I hate.

The War Reporter Paul Watson and the Barrel Bombs

The bird is really a spider spinning
miles overhead, dangling its dreadful sac
of water heaters, gas canisters or
rusted mufflers with stabilizing fins
soldered on—basically pieces-of-shit
IEDs of TNT, nitrogen
-rich fertilizer, diesel, anything
meant to keep burning after exploding
upon impact. Scrap metal for shrapnel
like candy inside piñatas. Released
into their comical, almost human
-like spiraling, affianced sky divers
flailing and clutching, until they align
in a bullet-nosed dive into the hum
-drum day below. Light, sound. The mushroom cloud
sashays. Then the nauseous smog of plastic
burning, blizzards of concrete. Low moaning
beneath counterfeit earth. The living look
like stereotyped Africans wearing
masks of white dust. Or debauched characters
in some sick comedy of manners. Limbs
like tangled marionettes. Children rescued
as a parody of birth, reviving
like fish thrown back to sea. An old man blinks
pantsless on what was his toilet, atoms
orbit away. Bits of spine, bits of spine
tossed on a blanket. A foot in a sock
sticks out of the mountain. They tickle her
to see if they should dig. We come for you,
he swears to the camera. By which he means
the killers, apparently, and not this
buried victim.

The War Reporter Paul Watson and the Boy with the Long Knife

He has terrible teeth in a wide smile
reflecting in the slim, serrated blade
in his sinister hand. A Dixie cup
of milk tea in the right. Casting a glance
over his shoulder, as if he's concerned
Assad is watching. Or the boy's father
if the father isn't dead. When instead
he ought to be hocking the oranges
that glisten and seem to breathe like the breasts
in his dreams. Or on the web, wherever
he can find them. While men on scooters skid
through last night's fallout. Bomb dust like pollen
fuzzing the light. The boy's knife is as long
as my forearm. So I show him the stump
of my hand: he laughs. Sheathing the weapon
in his elastic waistband. I ask, Why
do you need the knife? —Life, he smiles again,
of course. As a pair of boys shout, *Hello!*
Goodbye! marching in and out of the sun
hand in hand.

The War Reporter Paul Watson and the Girl
and the Mountain of Nothing

What's in the mountain of nothing? A girl
scrambling the summit with her eyes. Her mouth
hangs back. As if merely impressed. Wire mesh
in broken concrete like the antennae
of giant robot roaches. Quashed. While stairs
cascade sideways. Neighbors spinning their lives
out of vivisected bedrooms. These stones
like all the world's walls have been dismantled
and discarded over Homs. With coping
stones dashed, keystones unshrugged. Names and dates wiped
off cornerstones in the crash. *But my eyes*
adore the girl's clear-eyed stare. Like nothing
worth noting. Or looting. This collapsing
womb of stories. With friends inside. *This girl*
spins on her heel. Wearing blue jeans, outgrown
skirt on top. Hijab. A weathered bomber
coat like a trench. She holds a bag of bread
for someone, surely. Takes a step. A boy
striding past flips his hood up to the rain
and looks at me. Then up at the mountain
of nothing. To see what I see. *Nothing*
worth noting, or looting. Walk on.

The War Reporter and the Poet Fight

I sense we've depressed them, Dan. *Okay, Paul.*
This is Hollywood so they're expecting
Bang Bang, Combat Sex. *I know.* Radio
has this saying: Listeners don't listen
because they're too busy doing dishes
or taking a shit. *Okay.* And by now
executives will be wondering if
their wives are shtupping the pool boys. Then what
would you change? You've got to follow the way
the distracted mind works. Okay. I hear
like this circular saw in your driveway
gnawing—? Why don't we close the window then?
You're an actor onstage whose audience
will have stopped caring by now, Dan. I know
what an audience wants, Paul. Somebody
should kill somebody or—I'm not going to
do a tap dance for them! Okay. I won't
wear a lot of, I don't know, hats. Okay,
Dan, but still, you've got to *surprise* them! Let's
just try to get through this run-through once, Paul,
okay? Because I'm a good example
of somebody who can't pay attention
well. Ha ha ha. Ha ha ha. I feel that
your comments, Paul—Okay. About our pitch
have become kind of—What. Fear-based. They *are*
fear-based! Okay. My entire life is fear
-based, Dan! And my approach is to *repress*
fear, Paul! Okay, but just be ready when
they get bored. The reason they'll get bored is
because we can't get through like two minutes
of this pitch without you stopping to give
me fucking notes! I may be wrong and if
I am, well, sorry, but that reminds me

we need to inject more gallows humor
into this. Our task is to focus here,
Paul. Okay. Why don't we take a breather
and drink a glass of water, or maybe
something stronger? —Oh and also cut down
your intro, Dan. I'm just being myself,
Paul. Okay, but telling them you heard me
on the *radio*? What. Why don't you say
you had like this shotgun in your mouth and
I made you weep or something? You didn't
make me weep, though. What was the reason then
you first reached out to me? You know. Tell me
the reason. I've told you. But you've got to
move me, Dan! You've got to move me too, Paul!
Okay. And not go off on these tangents.
Okay. And you've got to keep track of time
because you don't have a very good sense
of time. I get that. And please stop talking
in like this shell-shocked monotone—I talk
in a monotone? You see this is what
I didn't want to do! But this is how
I talk, Dan! Okay. Why didn't you say
so before? Because I didn't want to
start a fight! But if you tell me today
I won't be boring tomorrow! I am
telling you now! Okay but I wasn't
getting it, Dan. Okay. I'm used to blunt
coworkers. I was exaggerating
because you pushed me. I need to be slapped
around, Dan. Paul, I feel like I'm getting
a lot of pressure here. No, no pressure
from me! What's important is that we try
to relax. Okay. And stop being scared
of scaring them. Okay. And that is why
you shouldn't be reading these how-to books

about Hollywood. You're right, I have been
in my head, Dan. You're scared. And I shouldn't
be reading that junk, it's junk! It's okay
if you're scared, I am too. I've been searching
for answers. And all we can do is say
we have this story and do you want to
help us sell it? Okay, Dan. Okay, Paul.
Let's do this again. Okay. And this time
if I'm boring I want you to hit me
with the truth.

The War Reporter Paul Watson and the Week of Taking Meetings

In the beginning the Executive
says sorry she's late. Her kids pitched a fit
on the PCH en route to day camp
in Malibu. Like a dominatrix
flanked by bearded masochists. *Mad Men*-style
glasses, impassive faces. I travelled
with the rebel side, says Paul. SCUD missiles
pulverizing apartment blocks. Digging
children out, mostly dead. I have some pics
if you'd like to see them? I can't even
begin to imagine! she cries. *Sorry*
to keep you waiting, says a homely blonde
who seems somehow already jilted and
her whiskey-voiced, whiskered hipster second
-in-command. Too many beards in the room!
japes the Poet. You're a poet? I feel
outclassed, winks Whiskey Beard. I went to grad
school for this? Sad Dumpy mopes. I forgot
to let my intern know what to order
for lunch, wait a sec. It's gallows humor,
says the War Reporter. If you enjoy
your jokes-on-a-rope then you'll like the world
of *The Zone.* Is that your tone? asks the Blonde
frowning. Sounds like a downer. Paul parries,
It's the new Rwanda! So everything
so far's been just backstory? He might be
bisexual, concedes the Poet. If
you don't have an idea then don't act like
you do. The room seems to sway. We don't know
what we don't know, do we? to paraphrase
Don Rumsfeld, Paul cracks. We're about to run

over, she says. Why don't we retire then
to the bar in the Cheesecake Factory?
floats Paul. Wow, she says, just wow and thank you
for coming in! We have glimpsed the future
and they're stupid, murmurs Paul. But one day
they'll die too, soothes the Poet. *You both look
like war reporters!* glad-hands another
young Turk, bearded, horn-rimmed glasses. Congrats
on the Emmy, I say. Thank you but when
you get into business with a name like
Name Redacted—! We're all feeling pretty
jazzed today. But the question is can we
do it all again? Which is where you two
jerks come in. Ha ha ha. I've always been
drawn to war, says Paul. Perhaps I'm jumping
the gun here, says Mr. Emmy. Your world's
great in terms of its scope, I get the soap
opera aspect here, but what's the story
of your Season One in just one word? Fish
-out-of-water, offers the Poet. Truth
-teller-in-exile, the War Reporter
says at the same time. Thanks and a pleasure
to have met you! Well that went pretty well,
says Paul. Considering he's a man. *A voice
via speakerphone.* Bry's at Comic-Con
in San Diego. Say hi, Bry. Hello,
Carrie! Greetings, guys. Are you cosplaying
as something in particular? Carrie
sasses her absent colleague. There's a guy
in the corner, bearded, glasses. Pardon?
answers the Voice of Bry. That's funny, laughs
the Cornered Exec. War has eternal
appeal, explains Paul. That Somalian kid
sporting our corpse's goggles while flashing
my camera the finger? burnt flesh on sticks?

teeth in handkerchiefs? Speaking to the dead
soldier I said—sorry, I get choked up
just talking about it, still. His children
have children now. Okay, any questions
then, Bryan? she asks. The Beard smiles. Bry-Bry,
you still there? Sorry, I must've muted
my end, ha ha ha, ha ha ha, great job
everybody! That lady looked sleepy,
says Paul in the lobby. Probably got kids
to pick up in Malibu. *Mazel tov!*
says another Blonde Executive when
she learns my wife is pregnant. I adore
poems—I promise! she crows. Reminding me
of a coxswain on the ladies' crew team
I once wrote sonnets for. I'm so sorry,
says Paul, breaking down as he swipes open
The Picture on his iPad. I wear this
paracord bracelet in case I get stuck
in a jam, he says. You never know when
you might need an instant noose! I love no
I appreciate—I mean this has been
just fabulous! Standing up. We'll sit down
internally and discuss. It's been real,
she smiles, and when's your baby due? Touching
wood. Ha ha ha! She cried! cries Paul. Real tears
pooled in her eyes! While the receptionist
validates our parking. Women tend to
cry more easily. Going down, going down,
he drones in the elevator. My shrink
works in this building, says the Poet. *Noon*
in a space-age solarium, two guys
with beards, glasses, like identical twins
who are secretly in love. Do we see
him kidnapped? beaten? tortured? Sure, says Paul.
Do you want to? I ask. There's nice Arabs,

and there's bad Arabs, Paul preaches. Because
The Zone's a morally ambiguous,
poisonous place. For instance, can we trust
who we're talking to right now? Will you kill
off any of our principal players?
they ask. Sure! says Paul. Would you like us to?
I ask. And is the idea that you two
would write this thing together? Sure! says Paul.
If you pay us to, I say. Well thank you
both for coming in. At the valet stand
in bleaching sun he says: I'm on the verge
of an actual breakdown. When they ask,
Does somebody get killed? they get to slump
into their screening rooms. To be really
real, he adds, the character who should die
is the one we like the most. So, sushi?
inquires the Poet. Ha ha ha. Text me
if you can't find the place. *A conference call*
a lifetime later with the Fixer, half
-Indian, via Princeton, who dresses
in a Silver Lake sort of way, skinny
jeans and high tops, flannel and a blazer
without much structure, audibly stroking
his fulsome beard, amber, Ashkenazi
eyes, sea-green, Grandpa on the Jewish side
invented backyard pools so he knows how
to parlez-vous the patois where subtext
can be hard to hold on to—So the news
is everybody passed. Nobody cares
about war, really. And while your story's
heartbreaking, Paul, truth is it would simply
cost too much. But let's touch base down the line
and try and set up another brunch.

The Poet's New Life

arrives like death in the night. And by dawn
we're engaged in the cardinal movements
of bringing forth light. *Dear God, deliver*
us from labor. We come crying hither
and alone, quoth the bard. Despite the noise
in this oceanside suite crowded with ghosts
of friends. Of warriors. Pulling back a leg
apiece. Erecting the tombstone-pillars
as we cradle her head. In agony
invoking your namesake. The body used
to tell a kind of story we'll only
ever have a hand in. As the doctor
rolls her fingers inside the widening
bowl of your mother's hips. Your skull's as big
as the moon in Tarot, but inverted
delightfully towards the stars. The cut
slits the dam, and out and up the salmon
leaps gasping and shitting onto the shore
of your mother's ardent breast. Soothing flesh
from breathless clay to bawling rose. Wide world
-eyed. Wall- then cross-eyed. The sweet off-key hymn
of women in empathy. Enemies
echo in your features, poor girl. Despite
a prize lost, a prize won, I hear the bell
of the beloved calling my name. Blessed
servants. Never alone. The dumb thunder
-clap of middle age has come.

The Former War Reporter Paul Watson

For the poetry and/or the drama:
I finally had my come-to-Jesus
convo with the bosses. Who I know now
are scum. Sending me this formal letter
insisting I desist from impugning
their reputation. —What reputation?
and a rimshot please. Might have to appear
with legal counsel pouring their poison
in my ear. When all I've done was inform
a few friends, mostly Afghans by the way,
I wouldn't be returning anytime
soon. How can I be? Without a promise
the bosses will have my back and do right
by my wife and son when I'm not around
to throw these tantrums. Whatever happened
to that inborn, inalienable right
to free speech which, if I'm not mistaken,
newspapers used to stand for? The old world
is older, and boy, do I feel stupid
for risking my life for so long. And boy
do I feel optimistic. An agent
in New York is reading my book treatment
on Arctic horror and/or another
forgotten history of the last time
we had a truly great war.

The Former War Reporter Paul Watson Goes to the Wrong Party

Bare bones: Jecca texted directions to
a soirée in SoHo. Millennials
in flannel, bearded, horn-rimmed, smoking pot
on the stoop. Out-of-character I asked,
Are you part of the party? They sent me
upstairs. Into this painted-white hallway
with numberless doors, cocking my ears for
the murmur of revelry. *In a loft*
stuffed with Coptic papyrus and tribal
statues of phalluses. Something that sounds
like ABBA on steroids. Everyone looks
apathetic. Like assholes. I elbow
my way to the bar, where open bottles
are empty. And find myself fingering
a quality cab sav, when this girl says,
That's not how you do it. Watch—this is how
it's done. Dipping and screwing and popping
my cork. Are you Jecca? I'm an actress,
she says, tapping her tip jar. I'd rather
be streaming *Breaking Bad* on my iPad
back at the hotel Jecca paid for, not
to mention the flight. So I give the room
one last look-see, and discover a man
even older than me, palavering
with some rouged patroness. Pardon me but
do either of you know Jecca? Is she
a lesbian? she asks. I have a son
named Declan, the old gent confides. I'm lost,
I say. Aren't I? Pearls-and-diamonds goes
to the bathroom. Camel-hair boasts, I saved
opera for Orlando! So I mention

my theory that God's a benefactor
of the arts. Then showing myself out, life
only becomes more mysterious as
I wander, snow falling like fat cinders
from Freedom Tower. Not even the wind
to sing for the dead I've known. I miss you
now more than ever, my friend. Write to me
if you can.

The Former War Reporter Paul Watson Finds It Beautiful

On the way home he stopped to see his mom
in the nursing home. She clung to his hand
and wouldn't let go. Without knowing who
he was, he was someone, surely. But first
breakfast. He fed her. Half-finished, she clawed
at him some more. Stared at his paw. She seemed
to be figuring this all out. He yawned
and she asked, Are you tired? I was tossing
and turning all night, he replied. Guilty
conscience, she smiled. Tut, tut, tut. Then drifting
back under the closing ice. Life is strange
sometimes because it's beautiful, he wrote.

The Former War Reporter Paul Watson Walks the Ledo Road

It was the road some said couldn't be built
through Himalayan jungles in monsoons
less lethal than mosquitos, clouds of mites
nibbling like piranhas, leeches sneaking
life from thighs, scrotums, behind ears in pools
of sucking mud, vines like the embraces
of neurotic mothers, the bloody burst
of tigers from branches. Unseen jaguars
phantasmal like Africa. While the Japs
zapped brimstone from above. White officers
like antebellum slave-drivers whipping
black GIs, metaphorically. While tires
swiveled down hopeless tracks, dragging more blacks
into abysses. *I know we didn't*
sell our show, Paul. I'm sorry. But maybe
we could write it anyway? Evelio's
the son of black Cubans who rolled cigars
in Ybor City. In photos his grin
is mischievous. Garrison-capped. He joked
about poker, pretty girls and cuddling
tent rats fatter than house cats. Weekend trips
to India for light bulbs, measuring
the road with a rusted surveyor's chain
for white superiors until he told them,
Jeeps have odometers, you know. Like me,
I tell Evelio, you're a professional
troublemaker. *I haven't heard from you*
in months. I hope you're safe. Isobel is
here, and healthy. Her mother too. Maybe
we could write something entirely new
together? Like India, the Chinese are
resurrecting the road. Pounding concrete
cobbles into dirt. When the rains sweep through

the road swells, then shrinks like glass. In India
it's just a footpath. Whereas the Chinese
border's a bazaar, traders and tourists
on their way to transsexual burlesques
in Myanmar. In between villagers
meander like Main Street. When the tremor
of an approaching truck drives them onto
the verge, they gawk at sojourners swaying
on benches, buckets. *It's probably good*
we move on. Because you can't keep doing
what you do, and I can't either. We turn
to climb a hill to Hla Di Lu. Whose key
dangles from a necklace of gruesome twine
and unlocks the padlock on her door where
somebody's spray-painted, Merry Xmas
and Happy New Year! Massaging memories
out of her brow. At her table. Blurring
eyes like a newborn. The Japanese ran
her father through with bayonets. Mother
raped in this paddy. Whereas the black men
twisted their fruit tins open for children
at the side of the road. *I'm losing you,*
Paul. Your voice. Where are you now? In a room
in Oakland hardly bigger than the bed
that holds Evelio. His hands like mallets,
leg amputated at the knee. His skin
like exhausted canvas. Whispering. Each word
is hard labor. In 1943
he wrote, *We'll have to try and make the best*
of whatever comes our way, till the day
we wake up from this nightmare. Close your eyes,
Evelio, the old road is coming back
to life. A strange light grows. As an alarm
rings the nurse into another room.